Intelligent By Design
Building Responsible Machine Learning Systems

TABLE OF CONTENTS

CHAPTER 1: INTRODUCTION TO MACHINE LEARNING 7
- 1.1 Introduction to Machine Learning Concepts 8
- 1.2 Classification of Artificial Intelligence 11
- 1.3 Evolution and Impact of Machine Learning 14
- 1.4 Fundamental Theories in Machine Learning 15

CHAPTER 2: MACHINE LEARNING SYSTEMS DESIGN 17
- 2.1 Design Principles for Scalable ML Systems 17
- 2.2 Architectural Patterns in ML Systems 18
- 2.3 Evaluating and Selecting ML Technologies 19

CHAPTER 3: MACHINE LEARNING SOLUTIONS ARCHITECTURE 21
- 3.1 Core Components of ML Architecture 21
- 3.2 Designing for Performance and Scalability 22
- 3.3 Best Practices in ML Architecture 23

CHAPTER 4: APPLICATIONS OF MACHINE LEARNING..........................26
- 4.1 Exploration of Various Industries and Their ML Applications..................................26
- 4.2 Case Studies of Successful ML Implementations 28
- 4.3 ROI and Impact Assessment of ML Projects 29

CHAPTER 5: IN-DEPTH EXPLORATION OF MACHINE LEARNING ALGORITHMS 32
- 5.1 Detailed Discussion of Different ML Algorithms...32
- 5.2 When and How to Use Specific ML Algorithms..34
- 5.3 Practical Examples and Case Studies 35

CHAPTER 6: EXPLORING OPEN-SOURCE LIBRARIES IN MACHINE LEARNING 38
- 6.1 Overview of Popular Open-Source ML Libraries 38
- 6.2 Comparative Analysis and Use Case Recommendations 40
- 6.3 Integration of Libraries into ML Workflows 41

CHAPTER 7: DATA ENGINEERING AND TRAINING DATA FOR MACHINE LEARNING 44
- 7.1 Strategies for Data Collection and Management 44
- 7.2 Preprocessing and Cleaning Training Data..46
- 7.3 Ensuring Data Quality and Integrity...47

CHAPTER 8: FEATURE ENGINEERING, MODEL DEVELOPMENT, AND MODEL DEPLOYMENT 50

8.1 Techniques in Feature Engineering 50
8.2 Strategies for Model Development 51
8.3 Best Practices in Model Deployment 53

CHAPTER 9: MANAGING INFRASTRUCTURE AND TOOLING FOR MLOPS 56

9.1 Infrastructure with Kubernetes for Container Orchestration 56
9.2 Scaling and Securing ML Applications 58
9.3 Advanced Techniques in MLOps 59

CHAPTER 10: OPENSOURCE PLATFORMS FOR MACHINE LEARNING ... 62

10.1 Overview of Open-Source ML Platforms 62
10.2 Setup and Customization of Open-Source ML Platforms 63
10.3 Community Support and Ecosystem 64

CHAPTER 11: USING AWS FOR ML SOLUTIONS 66

11.1 Utilizing AWS AI Services for Building ML Solutions 66
11.2 Best Practices for Leveraging AWS for ML 67
11.3 Case Studies and Practical Examples 69

CHAPTER 12: DATA SCIENCE FRAMEWORK FOR ML SERVICES 72

12.1 Setting Up Data Science Environment on AWS 72
12.2 Leveraging AWS ML Services for Data Science Projects 74
12.3 Managing Resources and Cost Optimization 75

CHAPTER 13: ENTERPRISE-LEVEL ML ARCHITECTURES 78

13.1 Architectural Patterns for Enterprise-Level ML Solutions 78
13.2 Integrating AWS ML Services into Enterprise Systems 79
13.3 Security, Compliance, and Scalability Considerations 81

CHAPTER 14: HUMAN DIMENSIONS OF ML GOVERNANCE, BIAS, AND PRIVACY 84

14.1 Understanding and Mitigating Bias in ML 84
14.2 Ethical Considerations and ML Governance 85
14.3 Ensuring Privacy and Data Protection in ML Systems 87

CHAPTER 15: THE NEW FRONTIERS OF GENERATIVE AI 90

15.1 Exploring the Capabilities of Generative AI 91
15.2 Impact of Generative AI on Industries 91
15.3 Ethical Considerations and Future Challenges in Generative AI 92

CONCLUSION..94
NOTES...95

Chapter 1: Introduction to Machine Learning

Machine Learning stands as one of the most significant technological advancements of the 21st century, a pivotal innovation that has reshaped industries and revolutionized our understanding of data's potential. At its essence, machine learning is a subset of artificial intelligence that endows systems with the capability to learn from data, identify patterns, and make decisions with minimal human intervention. It signifies a leap from traditional programming, where machines are not just coded to perform tasks; they are trained to use data to refine those tasks with each iteration.

The advent of big data has catalyzed the rise of machine learning. In an age where vast quantities of information are generated every second, the ability to harness this data for predictive analysis and automated decision making is invaluable. Machine learning algorithms thrive on this abundance of data, utilizing it to improve continuously and adaptively. From healthcare, where it aids in the diagnosis and treatment of diseases, to finance, where it powers complex trading systems, ML's applications are as diverse as they are transformative.

Central to machine learning's success is its interdisciplinary nature, drawing from fields such as statistics, mathematics, computer science, and domain specific knowledge. This confluence has spawned a variety of methods and approaches that enable machines to learn. These methodologies are underpinned by models – mathematical frameworks that are trained using data to represent the problem space. The training process involves adjusting model parameters to minimize errors, honing the model's accuracy over time.

The impact of machine learning can be felt in everyday life. Whether it's voice assistants that respond to vocal commands, recommendation systems that tailor content to individual preferences, or autonomous vehicles that navigate traffic, machine learning is the invisible force driving these innovations. It has not only augmented efficiency and productivity across sectors but has also opened new frontiers in research and development, pushing the boundaries of what's possible with technology.

Machine learning is not without its challenges, however. Issues such as data privacy, security, and ethical use are at the forefront of discussions surrounding its deployment. The need for large volumes of quality data to train models has raised questions about data governance and the potential for bias in decision making processes. As the field evolves, these challenges are increasingly being addressed through advancements in the technology itself, as well as through robust policies and frameworks that govern its use.

As we proceed with this book, we will focus on the architecture and design aspects of AI driven applications. We will explore the critical components of machine learning systems, including how they are structured and how they operate. The chapters will guide readers through the key elements of building AI applications, emphasizing practical approaches to designing systems that are not only intelligent but also scalable and efficient. Through this, we aim to equip readers with a solid understanding of the architectural foundations necessary for developing advanced machine learning applications.

1.1 Introduction to Machine Learning Concepts

Machine learning is a complex sector within artificial intelligence that grants computers the capability to process and learn from data, leading to autonomous decision-making. This influential technology is pivotal in shaping numerous facets of our modern lives, from routine daily activities to the advanced operations of industrial systems.

Central to machine learning is the deployment of sophisticated algorithms that meticulously examine data to discern patterns and relationships. These algorithms are adept at extracting insights from a multitude of data sources, enabling them to predict outcomes or make decisions that can have far-reaching implications. The learning mechanism involves feeding the system with various data forms, such as user interactions, sensor outputs, visual content, or textual information, which the system uses to refine its algorithms and improve its predictive accuracy over time.

One of the transformative aspects of machine learning is its dynamic adaptability, which eliminates the need for constant human oversight. It allows for the creation of systems that are not just rule-following entities but also predictive instruments capable of personalizing user experiences and optimizing complex processes.

Machine learning's impact is evident across multiple industries. In healthcare, it powers diagnostic tools for increased precision; in finance, it underpins systems for forecasting market trends; in transportation, it is the driving force behind the development of self-navigating vehicles; and in customer service, it enables chatbots and virtual assistants to provide nuanced support to users. These applications demonstrate machine learning's role in enhancing the accuracy and personalization of services and products.

At the core of machine learning is the development of intelligent, adaptive technology that evolves its functionality through data. This process, which requires minimal human intervention, changes the traditional role of humans from direct programmers to creators of environments conducive to machine learning.

As we explore the intricacies of machine learning, we will discover the inner workings of these algorithms, their diverse applications across industries, and their significant role in driving technological advancement and societal progress. Machine learning is not merely a tool but a driver of innovation, reshaping our interaction with technology and the broader environment.

1.1.1 Defining Machine Learning and Its Scope

Machine learning, though rooted in concepts that date back several decades, has become a buzzword synonymous with innovation in the digital age. It's a branch of artificial intelligence that infuses systems with the ability to learn from data, recognize patterns, and make decisions with varying degrees of autonomy. The expansion of machine learning is fueled by the digital revolution—characterized by an explosion of data, increased computing power, and advancements in algorithmic designs. The breadth of machine learning's application is remarkable, impacting virtually every facet of human life.

In the world of technology, machine learning is the silent workhorse behind the scenes, powering sophisticated search engine algorithms that we interact with every day. It's the intelligence behind the scenes that curates your social media feeds and online advertisements, ensuring that the content you see is tailored to your preferences. Furthermore, the automotive industry has been revolutionized by the advent of machine learning, with self-driving cars transitioning from science fiction to reality, navigating roads with increasing precision, and promising a future of enhanced safety and efficiency.

Beyond these highly visible applications, machine learning's versatility extends into the financial sector, where it's used to detect fraudulent activities, automate trading decisions, and personalize banking services. Healthcare has also seen significant advancements with machine learning, from new diagnostic methods and personalized treatment plans to managing patient data and streamlining operations. In education, machine learning algorithms provide personalized learning experiences, adapt resources to student needs, and even automate administrative tasks. The entertainment industry, too, leverages machine learning to analyze viewer preferences, optimize content delivery, and drive creative processes in filmmaking and game development.

The scope of machine learning is constantly expanding as researchers and practitioners discover new ways to apply its principles to solve problems and create value. It is a field characterized by relentless innovation, where today's breakthroughs lay the groundwork for tomorrow's everyday technology. Machine learning algorithms have begun to outperform humans in specific tasks, such as image and speech recognition, and are becoming increasingly sophisticated at tasks requiring cognitive capabilities.

Moreover, machine learning is reshaping the business landscape, providing companies with the tools to make smarter decisions, understand consumer behavior, and open up new markets. It has become a cornerstone in strategic decision-making, offering insights that drive competitive advantages. It has also transformed the way organizations operate, enabling more agile and responsive business models that can quickly adapt to changing market dynamics.

As we continue to generate and collect data at an unprecedented scale, the potential for machine learning only grows. It promises to unlock new frontiers in scientific research, such as decoding complex biological processes or tackling climate change by modeling environmental systems. The reach of machine learning is vast, and its potential is limited only by our ability to harness and direct its power toward beneficial ends. With its ever-expanding scope, machine learning is not just shaping our technology and industries but is also poised to redefine our understanding of intelligence, creativity, and innovation.

1.1.2 Core Principles of Machine Learning

Machine learning stands on the foundational principles that govern the way machines interact with, interpret, and learn from data. At the heart of these principles is the concept of autonomy in learning—the notion that a machine can independently sift through data, identify patterns, and make informed decisions. This is achieved through sophisticated algorithms, which are constructed not only to follow pre-set rules but also to develop an understanding of the data they process. This understanding enables them to adapt and improve their performance over time, a process reminiscent of human learning but executed at a scale and speed that humans cannot match.

These core principles are not static; they evolve as the field of machine learning itself advances. Initially, machine learning algorithms were simple and linear, designed to perform specific tasks where the relationship between input data and output decisions was straightforward. However, as the complexity of tasks and the volume of data have grown, the algorithms have become more complex, leveraging deep learning and neural networks to process information in ways analogous to the human brain.

The principles of machine learning also emphasize the importance of data quality and quantity. For a machine to learn effectively, it must have access to large, diverse, and high-quality datasets. The adage 'garbage in, garbage out' holds particularly true in machine learning—poor quality data can lead to inaccurate models that make poor decisions. Therefore, a significant part of machine learning involves preprocessing data to ensure its cleanliness, relevance, and suitability for the task at hand.

Another core principle is the ability of machine learning models to generalize from the data they are trained on. This means that after learning from a set of data, a machine learning model should be able to apply what it has learned to new, unseen data and still make accurate predictions or decisions. Achieving this generalizability is one of the most challenging aspects of machine learning, requiring careful algorithm design and rigorous model evaluation.

Machine learning also prioritizes efficiency, both in terms of computational resources and the time it takes for models to learn. Efficient algorithms can process larger datasets and learn more quickly, which is essential in a world where data is constantly being generated. This principle drives researchers to develop new machine learning methods that can operate at scale without compromising on speed or accuracy.

Finally, the deployment of machine learning models is guided by principles that ensure these models are integrated seamlessly into larger systems. This includes considerations of how the model will interact with other components, how it will be maintained and updated over time, and how its decisions can be explained to end-users. Deployability and maintainability are critical for the practical application of machine learning, ensuring that models remain useful and accurate as the world around them changes.

These core principles form the backbone of machine learning, guiding practitioners as they navigate the complexities of algorithm development, data management, and model deployment. As the field continues to grow, these principles will continue to be refined, leading to more advanced and capable machine learning systems.

1.1.3 Distinction Between AI and Machine Learning

The terms Artificial Intelligence and machine learning are frequently conflated, leading to confusion about their distinctions. AI is an overarching concept that embodies the pursuit of creating machines capable of mimicking human cognitive functions. It's a multidisciplinary science with multiple approaches, but advancements in machine learning and deep learning are creating a paradigm shift in virtually every sector of the tech industry. AI systems are designed to perform tasks ranging from the simple to the complex with a degree of intelligence that is often associated with human minds, such as learning, problem-solving, and decision-making.

Machine learning, a subset of AI, is specifically concerned with the algorithms and statistical models that enable computers to perform a task without using explicit instructions, relying instead on patterns and inference. It's about giving machines access to data and letting them learn for themselves. This self-learning aspect is what differentiates machine learning from traditional software—the ability of systems to not just follow a prescribed set of instructions but to dynamically adapt to new information and improve their own processing.

AI seeks to simulate a broad range of human cognitive abilities. This includes complex problem-solving skills, understanding natural language, recognizing objects and sounds, and responding to the environment in a way that mimics human responses. Machine learning, however, is more narrowly focused on developing algorithms that allow computers to learn how to perform tasks by analyzing data. These tasks could be as simple as identifying spam emails or as complex as diagnosing diseases from medical images.

While AI as a science is concerned with creating both narrow AI, which is designed to perform specific tasks, and general AI, which would outperform humans at nearly every cognitive task, machine learning remains one of the most effective ways to realize the former. Machine learning algorithms use vast amounts of data to train models that can recognize patterns and make predictions. Each time the algorithm processes a new piece of data, it adjusts its operations in an attempt to improve the accuracy of its predictions.

Deep learning, a further subset of machine learning, takes inspiration from the human brain, creating artificial neural networks that can learn from large amounts of complex data. These deep learning networks are capable of making some of the most significant advancements in AI, including highly accurate speech and image recognition, sophisticated language translation, and even the potential to create new, innovative content.

All machine learning is AI, but not all AI is machine learning. Machine learning is one way to achieve AI, focusing specifically on the learning aspect, where machines improve from access to data and experience. AI encompasses a broader array of technologies that also includes robotics, rule-based systems, and many other disciplines of computer science. As we continue to advance in the field, the distinction between AI and machine learning becomes even more nuanced, with machine learning driving many of the most exciting developments in AI today.

1.2 Classification of Artificial Intelligence

Artificial Intelligence stands as one of the most revolutionary and fast-evolving domains in the technological landscape. To better understand this complex and multifaceted field, it's crucial to delve into the various classifications of AI, each representing different levels of sophistication, capability, and potential impact. In this comprehensive overview, we will explore the distinct categories of AI – from Artificial Narrow AI to the speculative realms of Super AI and beyond. We will examine real-world examples and theoretical concepts that illustrate the functionalities and future possibilities of each AI type.

1.2.1 Artificial Narrow AI (Weak AI)

Example: Voice assistants like Siri or Alexa. These AI systems excel in performing specific tasks such as setting reminders, answering questions, or controlling smart home devices. They operate within a limited pre-defined range and can't handle tasks beyond their programming.

Significance: Narrow AI represents the current frontier of AI technology, demonstrating how machines can outperform humans in specific domains, such as playing chess or Go, or in image and speech recognition tasks.

1.2.2 Artificial General Intelligence (AGI, or Strong AI)

Theoretical Example: An AI with the intellectual capabilities of an average human adult. It could learn to cook a new recipe, write a poem, or solve a complex mathematical problem without prior explicit programming in each of these domains.

Significance: AGI remains a theoretical concept. Its realization would mark a paradigm shift in AI, where machines can perform any intellectual task that a human can, with the ability to transfer learning across a wide range of unrelated tasks.

1.2.3 Artificial Super AI

Hypothetical Example: An AI that not only mimics but exceeds human intelligence, perhaps creating new scientific theories or art forms that are beyond human comprehension or capability.

Significance: Super AI is purely speculative and raises philosophical and ethical questions about machines surpassing human intellectual and emotional capacities.

1.2.4 AI Functionalities

AI functionalities refer to the varying capabilities of artificial intelligence systems, each showcasing different levels of complexity and application. In this context, we explore two key functionalities: Reactive Machine AI and Limited Memory AI.

Reactive Machine AI

Reactive Machine AI represents one of the most basic types of AI functionalities. These systems are designed to respond to specific inputs without any learning capability or memory of past actions. They excel in structured environments where responses are predictable and do not require past experience.

Example: A prime example of Reactive Machine AI is IBM's Deep Blue, the chess-playing computer that famously defeated world champion Garry Kasparov in 1997. Deep Blue was programmed to analyze the chessboard, evaluate millions of possible moves, and predict outcomes based on its current state. Unlike humans, it didn't rely on past games or learning from previous experiences; it made decisions purely based on real-time analysis and pre-programmed strategies.

Significance: The success of Deep Blue in chess, a game with well-defined rules and outcomes, underscores the capability of Reactive Machine AI in excelling at specific tasks. These systems demonstrate how machines can process information and make decisions with a level of efficiency and accuracy that is challenging for humans, especially in tasks that involve complex calculations or rapid processing of large datasets.

Limited Memory AI

Limited Memory AI takes a step further by incorporating the ability to use historical data to inform decisions. These systems can look back at recent actions or data inputs to make better-informed decisions.

Example: Self-driving cars epitomize Limited Memory AI. These vehicles use AI to process a combination of historical data and real-time sensor inputs. The historical data might include information from past trips, such as routes, traffic patterns, and navigation experiences, which inform the AI's current decision-making process. Simultaneously, real-time data from cameras, LIDAR, and other sensors allow the vehicle to navigate, recognize obstacles, and adjust to changing road conditions.

Significance: Limited Memory AI demonstrates a significant advancement in the field of artificial intelligence by showing how the integration of past experiences can enhance decision-making in dynamic and unpredictable environments. This type of AI is pivotal in applications where immediate context and historical information are both crucial for accurate and efficient decision-making. It marks a step toward more advanced AI systems that can learn and adapt over time, paving the way for more autonomous and intelligent machines capable of handling complex, real-world tasks.

1.2.5 Theoretical AI Capabilities

Theoretical AI capabilities represent the cutting-edge concepts and future possibilities in the realm of artificial intelligence. Two significant areas in this domain are the Theory of Mind AI (also known as Emotion AI) and Self-Aware AI. These concepts push the boundaries of AI's capabilities far beyond current technological realities, venturing into realms that blur the lines between machines and humans.

Theory of Mind AI (Emotion AI)

Theory of Mind AI refers to the development of AI systems that can understand, interpret, and respond to human emotions. This capability goes beyond mere data processing to encompass a nuanced understanding of human psychological states.

In Development Example: AI technologies are currently being developed to recognize and interpret human emotions through various methods, including analyzing facial expressions, voice intonations, and body language. For instance, AI systems in development for customer service applications use voice and speech analysis to detect customer frustration or satisfaction, allowing for more empathetic and effective responses.

Significance: The development of Emotion AI represents a significant leap in the field of human-AI interaction. It paves the way for AI systems that can engage with humans more naturally and effectively, catering to emotional needs and nuances. This capability is particularly valuable in applications like mental health assessment, customer service, and social robotics, where understanding and responding to human emotions is crucial. Emotion AI underscores the potential for AI to become more integrated and responsive within human-centric environments.

Self-Aware AI

Self-Aware AI is a hypothetical concept that envisages AI systems possessing their own consciousness, awareness of their existence, emotions, and needs.

Hypothetical Example: Imagine an AI that not only processes information and makes decisions but also has self-awareness and consciousness. Such an AI would be able to understand its existence independently, have subjective experiences, and possibly even have emotional states or desires that guide its actions.

Significance: The idea of Self-Aware AI raises profound philosophical, ethical, and technical questions. It challenges our understanding of consciousness and blurs the distinction between sentient beings and machines. The ethical implications of creating such entities are vast, raising questions about rights, responsibilities, and the moral status of AI. While still firmly in the realm of science fiction, this concept invites us to ponder the future trajectory of AI development and its potential impact on society.

The categorization of AI into capabilities (Narrow AI, AGI, Super AI) and functionalities (Reactive Machine AI, Limited Memory AI, Emotion AI, Self-Aware AI) provides a comprehensive framework for understanding the broad spectrum of AI's evolution. From current practical applications to speculative future possibilities, this framework offers insight into the dynamic and ever-evolving nature of AI, highlighting its potential to revolutionize our world in ways we are just beginning to imagine.

1.3 Evolution and Impact of Machine Learning

The field of machine learning has experienced an extraordinary evolution, from its early theoretical foundations to its current status as a cornerstone of modern technology and innovation. This journey, marked by groundbreaking developments and significant milestones, has reshaped our understanding of what machines are capable of achieving. The impact of machine learning extends far beyond the confines of technology; it influences economic patterns, societal structures, and even the minutiae of daily life. In this section, we explore the fascinating evolution of machine learning, tracing its historical roots, highlighting its major breakthroughs, and examining its profound societal and economic impacts. This exploration not only provides insights into how machine learning has become an integral part of our world but also offers a lens through which to view its future trajectory and the potential challenges and opportunities that lie ahead.

1.3.1 Historical Development of Machine Learning

The journey of machine learning began in the era of classical philosophers who attempted to describe human thinking as a symbolic system, but its modern incarnation started in the 1950s with the advent of computers. Alan Turing, a pioneer in computing and artificial intelligence, proposed the question "Can machines think?", which set the stage for the development of machine learning. The first computer learning program, the checker-playing program developed by Arthur Samuel in 1959, demonstrated the potential of machines to learn from experience. In the decades that followed, progress in ML was intermittent, marked by the ebb and flow of enthusiasm in the field known as "AI winters," due to challenges in computational power and data availability.

The resurgence of machine learning came with the internet boom and the exponential increase in data production and computational capabilities. The development of algorithms that could learn from large amounts of data without being explicitly programmed to perform specific tasks became a significant focus. Support vector machines, decision trees, and neural networks began to evolve, setting the groundwork for more sophisticated machine learning algorithms.

1.3.2 Breakthroughs and Milestones in Machine Learning

Machine learning has seen a number of breakthroughs and milestones that have accelerated its growth and application. A pivotal moment occurred when IBM's Deep Blue defeated world chess champion Garry Kasparov in 1997, showcasing the potential of ML in strategy and problem-solving. The introduction of the backpropagation algorithm allowed neural networks to learn from their errors, vastly improving their performance. This gave rise to deep learning, which mimics the neural structure of the human brain and has been instrumental in advancing the field.

The victory of Google's AlphaGo over the world champion in the board game Go in 2016 demonstrated that ML could tackle tasks of intuition and complexity previously thought beyond the reach of machines. The development of convolutional neural networks has revolutionized image recognition, leading to advancements in computer vision that enable applications like facial recognition and autonomous driving. Natural language processing has also benefited from ML, with models like GPT-3 showing the ability to generate human-like text, opening new possibilities in human-machine interaction.

1.3.3 The Societal and Economic Impact of Machine Learning

The societal and economic impact of machine learning is profound, affecting nearly every aspect of modern life. In the economic sphere, ML has driven innovation, creating new markets and transforming existing ones. It has become a critical driver of competitive advantage, with businesses leveraging ML for predictive analytics, customer service, and decision-making. This has led to more personalized services, efficient operations, and the birth of entirely new industries centered around data science and AI technologies.

On the societal front, machine learning has had a diverse impact. It has the potential to solve some of the most pressing global challenges, such as climate change and healthcare. ML algorithms are being used to optimize energy consumption, develop new materials, and analyze climate data to predict changes more accurately. In healthcare, ML is enabling personalized medicine, early detection of diseases, and streamlining hospital operations to improve patient care.

However, the rapid evolution of machine learning also presents challenges, particularly in the realms of privacy, security, and employment. The ability of ML to process vast amounts of personal data raises concerns about data protection and surveillance. There is also a growing discourse on the future of work as ML and AI continue to automate tasks traditionally performed by humans.

The impact of machine learning will continue to be a subject of critical analysis as the technology becomes further integrated into the fabric of society. It offers immense potential for positive change but also requires careful consideration of ethical, legal, and social implications. As machine learning becomes increasingly sophisticated, it is crucial to guide its evolution in a direction that maximizes societal benefit while mitigating risks.

1.4 Fundamental Theories in Machine Learning

The realm of machine learning is anchored in a rich tapestry of fundamental theories that form the bedrock of its practices and applications. These theories, a blend of insights drawn from diverse disciplines such as mathematics, statistics, computer science, and cognitive science, provide the essential framework for understanding how machines can be trained to learn from data, make predictions, and adapt to new information. This section delves into the intricate theoretical underpinnings of machine learning, uncovering the foundational concepts that have driven the field's rapid development. From exploring the mathematical constructs that enable machines to process and interpret data, to examining the core algorithms and model theories that facilitate machine learning, this section offers a comprehensive overview of the critical principles and ideas at the heart of this transformative technology. Understanding these fundamental theories is crucial for both practitioners and enthusiasts of machine learning, as it not only enhances one's grasp of the field but also empowers the development and refinement of more advanced and efficient learning algorithms.

1.4.1 Theoretical Foundations of Machine Learning

Machine learning, at its core, is built on a foundation of theories that blend concepts from computer science, statistics, and mathematics. These theoretical foundations provide the framework for understanding how machines can learn from and make predictions based on data. The roots of machine learning can be traced back to the theory of computation and algorithmic efficiency, which lays the groundwork for understanding the computational aspects of learning algorithms. The field also heavily draws from statistical theory, particularly the concepts of inference and probability, which help in making predictions and decisions from data. Additionally, information theory plays a crucial role in understanding and quantifying the amount of information in data, which is essential for effective learning.

1.4.2 Key Mathematical Concepts in ML

Several key mathematical concepts form the backbone of machine learning algorithms. Central among these is linear algebra, which provides a language for describing and manipulating data in the form of vectors and matrices. This is crucial in almost all areas of machine learning, from simple linear regression to complex neural networks. Calculus, particularly the concept of derivatives and gradients, is another fundamental aspect, especially in optimization algorithms used in training models. Concepts from probability and statistics are vital for understanding and modeling the uncertainty inherent in data and predictions. These include probability distributions, expectation and variance, and the Bayesian framework, which is fundamental to many supervised learning algorithms.

1.4.3 Understanding Learning Algorithms and Model Theory

Understanding machine learning also involves comprehending the theories behind various learning algorithms and models. This includes the distinction between supervised and unsupervised learning, where the former involves learning a function that maps input to output based on example input-output pairs, while the latter finds hidden patterns or intrinsic structures in input data. The concept of overfitting, where a model learns the detail and noise in the training data to the extent that it negatively impacts the performance of the model on new data, is also crucial. Additionally, the trade-offs between bias and variance, generalization ability, and the complexity of models are key considerations in the theory of machine learning.

Model theory in machine learning encompasses the structure of models and how they are designed to learn from data. This includes understanding different types of models such as decision trees, neural networks, support vector machines, and ensemble methods, and the contexts in which they are best applied. The theory also delves into the concept of model selection – choosing the right model for the right task – and model evaluation, which involves techniques to assess the performance of a machine learning model.

The fundamental theories in machine learning provide the necessary framework for understanding how machines can be taught to learn from data, make predictions, and improve over time. These theories are vital for anyone looking to delve deep into the field of machine learning, providing the tools to develop new algorithms, improve existing ones, and apply them effectively to solve real-world problems.

Chapter 2: Machine Learning Systems Design

In the dynamic and ever-evolving landscape of machine learning, the design of systems stands as a critical component that determines the success and efficiency of ML implementations. This chapter delves into the intricate process of crafting robust, scalable, and effective machine learning systems, which requires a harmonious blend of technical knowledge, strategic planning, and practical execution. This section is dedicated to unraveling the complexities involved in designing machine learning systems, offering insights into the principles and practices that guide the creation of these sophisticated systems. From the architectural frameworks that support machine learning operations to the strategic considerations necessary for deploying and maintaining these systems in real-world scenarios, this section provides a comprehensive guide for navigating the challenges and opportunities in the field of machine learning system design. Whether you're an aspiring data scientist, a seasoned ML engineer, or a business leader looking to leverage machine learning, understanding the nuances of system design is pivotal for harnessing the full potential of this groundbreaking technology.

2.1 Design Principles for Scalable ML Systems

In the rapidly advancing world of machine learning, the ability to scale systems efficiently is as crucial as the algorithms themselves. This section is a focused exploration into the methodologies and frameworks essential for building machine learning systems that are not only robust and high-performing but can also gracefully scale in response to varying demands. This section delves into the critical aspects of system architecture that enable scalability, discussing the strategies that facilitate the growth of machine learning systems without compromising their performance or efficiency. From understanding how to structure scalable architectures to balancing the intricate interplay between performance and scalability, and ensuring cost-effectiveness, this section provides a comprehensive guide for anyone looking to design and implement scalable machine learning solutions. As machine learning applications continue to grow in complexity and size, these design principles become indispensable for creating systems that can adapt and thrive in an ever-changing technological landscape.

2.1.1 Strategies for Building Scalable ML Architectures

Building scalable machine learning architectures is a strategic task that requires careful planning and execution. The key lies in creating systems that can efficiently handle increases in workload and data volume without compromising performance. One effective strategy is to employ modular designs where components of the ML system, such as data preprocessing, model training, and inference, can be scaled independently. This modular approach facilitates easier updates and maintenance. Additionally, leveraging cloud computing resources can provide the flexibility to scale resources up or down as needed. Another critical strategy is to utilize distributed computing, where tasks are divided and processed in parallel across multiple machines or nodes, significantly speeding up data processing and model training times.

2.1.2 Balancing Performance and Scalability in ML Systems

Achieving a balance between performance and scalability in machine learning systems is crucial. Performance, in terms of accuracy and speed of predictions, should not be sacrificed for the sake of scalability. Efficient data management techniques, such as data sharding and indexing, can ensure quick access to relevant data, improving performance. In terms of model design, choosing the right algorithm that suits the scale of the data while providing accurate results is essential. Sometimes, simpler models can yield better performance and scalability compared to more complex ones. Regular performance testing and monitoring can help identify bottlenecks and areas for improvement.

2.1.3 Cost-Effective Scalable Solutions in ML

Developing cost-effective scalable solutions in machine learning involves optimizing the use of computational resources to keep expenses in check. One way to achieve this is through efficient data and model management. For instance, using data compression and selecting relevant features can reduce the volume of data processed and stored, thereby saving costs. Another approach is to employ auto-scaling in cloud environments, where computing resources are automatically adjusted based on the system's load, ensuring that you pay only for the resources you use. Additionally, open-source tools and frameworks can significantly reduce software costs while providing high-quality, community-supported solutions for machine learning tasks.

Designing scalable ML systems requires a strategic approach that considers not just the technical aspects but also the cost implications. By focusing on modular, performance-optimized, and cost-efficient designs, organizations can build ML systems that are not only scalable but also sustainable in the long term.

2.2 Architectural Patterns in ML Systems

The design of machine learning systems is both an art and a science, requiring a deep understanding of various architectural patterns that can be employed. These patterns serve as blueprints guiding the structure, components, and behavior of ML systems. This section is a comprehensive exploration into the diverse frameworks and structures that underpin successful machine learning systems. This section will examine common architectural frameworks in ML, provide real-world case studies of successful ML system architectures, and discuss how these architectural patterns can be adapted for different ML applications. Understanding these patterns is crucial for building efficient, robust, and scalable ML systems that meet specific project requirements.

2.2.1 Common Architectural Frameworks in ML

There are several architectural frameworks commonly used in machine learning, each offering distinct advantages and suited to different types of ML tasks.

Layered Architecture: This is a widely used framework where different layers of the system are responsible for distinct aspects of the ML process, such as data preprocessing, feature extraction, model training, and output generation. This separation allows for modularity and ease of maintenance.

Microservices Architecture: In this approach, the ML system is divided into small, independent services that communicate over well-defined APIs. This pattern is highly scalable and allows different components of the ML system to be developed and deployed independently.

Pipeline Architecture: This framework structures the ML system as a series of stages or steps, where the output of one stage becomes the input for the next. It's particularly effective for managing complex data workflows and is widely used in data preprocessing and feature engineering tasks.

2.2.2 Case Studies: Successful ML System Architectures

Understanding architectural patterns in ML systems is enhanced by examining real-world applications. Several case studies illustrate how different architectures have been successfully implemented:

Layered Architecture in Image Recognition: A common implementation in computer vision, where layers are dedicated to tasks like edge detection, object recognition, and object classification.

Microservices in E-commerce Recommendations: Online retail giants often employ microservices to handle different aspects of recommendation systems, such as user preference modeling, product categorization, and personalized recommendation generation.

Pipeline Architecture in Natural Language Processing (NLP): Many NLP applications use pipeline architecture for tasks like tokenization, part-of-speech tagging, parsing, and semantic analysis.

2.2.3 Adapting Architectural Patterns for Different ML Applications

The choice of architectural pattern greatly depends on the specific requirements of the ML application. Factors such as the type of data, the complexity of the model, scalability needs, and deployment considerations dictate the most suitable architecture.

Scalability: For applications requiring scalability, microservices or cloud-based architectures are often preferred.

Real-time Processing: Systems needing real-time data processing, such as autonomous vehicles or fraud detection systems, may opt for architectures that prioritize speed and low-latency.

Complex Data Workflows: Applications with complex data workflows, such as those in biomedical research or financial forecasting, can benefit from pipeline architectures that manage the flow of data through multiple processing stages.

The choice of an architectural pattern in ML systems is a critical decision that influences the system's performance, scalability, and maintainability. By understanding and adapting these patterns to specific applications, ML practitioners can design systems that effectively meet the demands of their ML tasks.

2.3 Evaluating and Selecting ML Technologies

The rapidly evolving landscape of machine learning technologies presents both opportunities and challenges when it comes to selecting the right tools and platforms for ML projects. This section is a critical exploration into the methodologies and considerations involved in making informed decisions about the technological backbone of ML systems. This section delves into the criteria for technology selection, conducts a comparative analysis of existing ML technologies, and discusses strategies for future-proofing ML system designs with emerging technologies. Understanding these elements is essential for practitioners to build effective, efficient, and forward-looking ML solutions.

2.3.1 Criteria for Technology Selection in ML Projects

Selecting the right technology for ML projects involves a nuanced understanding of several key factors:

Project Requirements: The nature of the project, including its scope, complexity, and specific goals, often dictates the technology needed. For instance, deep learning projects might require different tools compared to simpler machine learning tasks.

Data Compatibility and Scalability: The chosen technology must be compatible with the data formats used and capable of handling the volume and velocity of data both currently and as the project scales.

Ease of Use and Flexibility: Tools that offer user-friendly interfaces and flexible options for customization can significantly reduce development time and improve productivity.

Performance and Efficiency: Evaluate the performance of technologies, especially in terms of processing speed, accuracy, and resource consumption.

Integration and Compatibility: Consider how well the technology integrates with existing systems and workflows.

Support and Community: A strong developer community and comprehensive support resources can be invaluable for troubleshooting and keeping pace with new developments.

2.3.2 Comparative Analysis of ML Technologies

Comparing ML technologies requires a deep dive into their features, strengths, and limitations. This analysis could involve:

Comparing Frameworks: Tools like TensorFlow, PyTorch, and Scikit-learn have different strengths – TensorFlow's extensive ecosystem and scalability, PyTorch's ease of use and dynamic computation graphs, and Scikit-learn's simplicity for beginners.

Platform Capabilities: Cloud platforms like AWS, Azure, and Google Cloud offer different ML services, each with unique features. Their comparison might focus on aspects like the range of services, cost, performance, and ease of deployment.

Specialized Tools: For certain applications, specialized tools or libraries might be necessary, such as OpenCV for computer vision or NLTK and SpaCy for natural language processing.

2.3.3 Futureproofing ML System Designs with Emerging Technologies

Future-proofing ML system designs is about staying adaptable and relevant in the face of rapidly advancing technology:

Embracing Modularity: Design systems with modularity, allowing for easy updates and integration of new technologies as they emerge.

Investing in Interoperability: Focus on technologies that promote interoperability, ensuring that the system can work with future technologies and standards.

Staying Informed: Keep abreast of emerging trends and breakthroughs in ML, such as advancements in quantum computing, AI ethics, or novel algorithmic approaches.

Training and Skill Development: Encourage continuous learning and skill development within teams to adapt to new technologies swiftly.

Evaluating and selecting the right ML technologies is a multifaceted process that demands careful consideration of a range of factors. By thoroughly assessing needs, comparing available options, and planning for future developments, ML practitioners can create systems that are not only effective today but also positioned to evolve with the advancing frontiers of technology.

Chapter 3: Machine Learning Solutions Architecture

In the rapidly advancing field of machine learning, the architecture of solutions plays a pivotal role in determining their success and efficacy. This chapter is a comprehensive exploration into the design, structure, and implementation of systems that harness the power of machine learning. This chapter provides a deep dive into the intricate world of ML architectures, offering insights into how these systems are conceptualized, developed, and deployed to solve real-world problems. From understanding the basic building blocks of ML systems to exploring advanced architectural frameworks, this chapter aims to equip readers with the knowledge and tools necessary for crafting robust and effective machine learning solutions. Whether it's for predictive analytics, natural language processing, computer vision, or any other application, the architecture of an ML solution is foundational to its functionality, scalability, and performance. This chapter serves as a guide for anyone looking to delve into the architectural aspects of machine learning, providing a roadmap for navigating the complexities of this dynamic and transformative field.

3.1 Core Components of ML Architecture

The architecture of a machine learning system is akin to the blueprint of a building; it lays out the essential components and their interactions, ensuring the system functions as intended. In this section, we explore the fundamental aspects that constitute the backbone of any ML system. This section is divided into three key areas: identifying the basic elements integral to ML system architecture, understanding the integration of data pipelines, and recognizing the significance of model management. Each component plays a crucial role in the efficiency, scalability, and overall success of ML projects, making this exploration crucial for anyone involved in the design and implementation of machine learning systems.

3.1.1 Fundamental Elements of ML System Architecture

The architecture of an ML system is built upon several fundamental elements:

Data Storage and Retrieval: The foundation of any ML system is data. Efficient data storage and retrieval mechanisms are crucial, as they determine how quickly and effectively the system can access the data it needs to learn and make predictions.

Processing Units: These are the computational cores of ML systems, responsible for executing the algorithms. They can range from general purpose CPUs to specialized hardware like GPUs or TPUs, which are optimized for the heavy computational demands of ML tasks.

Algorithms and Learning Models: The choice of algorithms and models is a core component that dictates how the system learns from data. This includes everything from simple linear regression models to complex deep learning neural networks.

User Interface and Reporting Tools: For ML systems to be practical, they need interfaces for users to interact with the system and tools to report and visualize the results of the ML process.

3.1.2 Integrating Data Pipelines in ML Architecture

Data pipelines are integral to the functionality of ML architectures. They involve several stages:

Data Collection: This is the process of gathering data from various sources, which can include databases, sensors, or user inputs.

Data Cleaning and Preprocessing: Raw data is rarely in a format ready for analysis. This stage involves transforming and normalizing data to a usable format.

Feature Engineering: This is where data scientists determine which aspects of the data are important and how they can be used to predict outcomes.

The integration of these pipelines must be seamless and efficient, ensuring a constant and consistent flow of data through the system.

3.1.3 Role of Model Management in ML Architecture

Model management is a critical component of ML architecture, involving several key processes:

Model Training: This process involves using data to train ML models. It requires robust computational resources and efficient algorithms.

Model Evaluation and Selection: After training, models must be evaluated to determine their accuracy and effectiveness. This often involves comparing multiple models to select the best performer.

Model Deployment: Once a model is selected, it needs to be deployed into a production environment where it can start making predictions or decisions based on new data.

Model Monitoring and Updating: Deployed models must be continuously monitored for performance and periodically updated or retrained with new data to ensure they remain accurate and relevant.

Understanding the core components of ML architecture is essential for building efficient and effective machine learning systems. Each element, from data management to model deployment, plays a crucial role in the system's overall performance and must be carefully considered and integrated within the broader architecture.

3.2 Designing for Performance and Scalability

In the realm of machine learning, the twin goals of performance and scalability are paramount. This section examines the strategies and considerations necessary to build ML systems that are not only fast and efficient but can also handle growth and larger datasets. Performance in ML systems refers to the speed and accuracy of the algorithms, while scalability pertains to a system's ability to maintain or improve performance as the size of the dataset grows. This section is divided into exploring techniques for enhancing performance, strategies for scaling ML systems, and finding the optimal balance between speed and accuracy.

3.2.1 Techniques for High Performance ML Systems

Developing high performance ML systems involves several key techniques:

Optimized Algorithms: Selecting and finetuning algorithms that are efficient and wellsuited to the specific task at hand is crucial. This includes choosing the right model complexity and using advanced optimization techniques.

Efficient Data Preprocessing: Reducing the size of the dataset through techniques such as feature selection and dimensionality reduction can significantly speed up processing times.

Parallel Processing and Hardware Acceleration: Utilizing GPUs (Graphics Processing Units) or TPUs (Tensor Processing Units) for parallel processing can drastically improve the training and inference times of ML models.

Caching and In-Memory Computing: Storing frequently accessed data in memory rather than fetching it from slower storage mediums can reduce latency and increase throughput.

3.2.2 Scaling ML Systems for Large Datasets
As datasets grow, scaling ML systems becomes a critical challenge:

Distributed Computing: Implementing distributed computing frameworks, such as Apache Spark or Hadoop, allows ML tasks to be processed across multiple machines, handling larger datasets more effectively.

Cloud Based Solutions: Leveraging cloud platforms can provide scalable resources on demand, ensuring that the system can adapt to varying data loads without the need for significant upfront hardware investment.

Data Sharding: Dividing large datasets into smaller, manageable chunks (shards) can improve processing speed and efficiency.

3.2.3 Balancing Speed and Accuracy in ML Designs
Finding the right balance between speed and accuracy is crucial for practical ML systems:

Model Complexity: While more complex models may offer higher accuracy, they can be slower to train and infer. Choosing the right model complexity for the task and available resources is essential.

Batch Processing vs. Real Time Processing: Depending on the application, it may be more efficient to process data in batches rather than in real time, trading off some degree of immediacy for improved speed and reduced computational load.

Testing and Validation: Rigorous testing and validation are required to ensure that any gains in speed do not come at the cost of reduced accuracy or model performance.

Designing ML systems for performance and scalability involves a multifaceted approach that considers the technical aspects of machine learning, from the algorithms and hardware used to the data management strategies. By striking the right balance between performance and scalability, ML practitioners can build systems that are both efficient and capable of handling the growing demands of big data and complex ML tasks.

3.3 Best Practices in ML Architecture
Crafting an effective machine learning architecture demands more than just a deep understanding of algorithms and data; it requires a strategic approach that adheres to best practices. This section focuses on the guidelines and methodologies that constitute the backbone of successful ML systems. This section delves into the essential aspects of creating robust ML architectures, ensuring flexibility and modularity, and incorporating crucial elements like security and compliance. These best practices are

pivotal in building ML systems that are not only efficient and accurate but also secure, adaptable, and sustainable over time.

3.3.1 Guidelines for Robust ML Architectural Design

Developing a robust ML architecture involves several key guidelines:

Clear Objective Definition: Begin with a clear understanding of the problem and the objectives of the ML system. This clarity guides the choice of algorithms, data sets, and system design.

Data-Centric Approach: Prioritize data quality over model complexity. Reliable and relevant data is essential for training effective models.

Scalable and Maintainable Code: Write code that is scalable, maintainable, and well-documented. This practice ensures that the system can evolve and adapt over time without becoming unwieldy.

Regular Evaluation and Testing: Implement continuous evaluation and testing of the model to ensure its accuracy and relevance. Use metrics that align with the system's objectives and make adjustments as needed.

Efficient Resource Management: Optimize the use of computational resources to balance performance with cost-effectiveness. Utilize cloud resources where appropriate for scalability.

3.3.2 Ensuring Flexibility and Modularity in ML Systems

Flexibility and modularity are critical in ML systems for several reasons:

Adaptability to Change: Flexible and modular systems can easily adapt to changes in data, objectives, or technology, without requiring a complete overhaul.

Ease of Experimentation: Modular systems allow for easy experimentation with different algorithms and techniques in isolated components without impacting the entire system.

Simpler Maintenance and Upgrades: Modularity makes maintenance and upgrades more manageable, as changes can be made to individual components without affecting the entire architecture.

3.3.3 Incorporating Security and Compliance in ML Architecture

Security and compliance are often overlooked but are crucial elements in ML architecture:

Data Privacy and Protection: Implement robust data privacy measures to protect sensitive information. Adhere to regulations like GDPR for data handling.

Secure Model Training and Deployment: Ensure the security of ML models during training and deployment phases. Protect against vulnerabilities that could be exploited.

Compliance with Ethical Standards: Adhere to ethical standards in AI and ML, ensuring that the models are fair, unbiased, and transparent.

Regular Security Audits: Conduct regular security audits to identify and address potential vulnerabilities in the system.

Adhering to best practices in ML architecture is essential for the success and sustainability of ML projects. By focusing on robust design, flexibility, modularity, security, and compliance, ML practitioners can create systems that are not only high-performing but also secure, adaptable, and ethical. These practices form the cornerstone of responsible and effective ML system development.

Chapter 4: Applications of Machine Learning

In the modern era, machine learning has transcended academic theory to become a pivotal force driving innovation across various sectors. This chapter is an expansive exploration into the diverse and ever-growing range of practical uses for ML in today's world. This journey into the realm of applied ML reveals how these sophisticated algorithms are no longer confined to the boundaries of research labs but are actively reshaping industries, transforming business practices, and influencing daily life. From automating routine tasks to solving complex problems that have long eluded human capabilities, ML applications are at the forefront of technological advancement and digital transformation.

This section unveils the breadth and depth of ML applications, illustrating how they have become integral in fields as varied as healthcare, finance, transportation, entertainment, and beyond. In healthcare, ML is revolutionizing diagnostics and patient care, offering predictions and insights that enhance treatment and save lives. In the world of finance, it provides the backbone for complex decision-making processes, from fraud detection to algorithmic trading. The transportation sector has witnessed a paradigm shift with the advent of autonomous vehicles and intelligent traffic management systems, all powered by ML algorithms.

Moreover, the entertainment industry has been transformed by ML, which now drives content recommendation engines and personalizes user experiences in ways previously unimaginable. In the realm of retail and e-commerce, machine learning optimizes supply chains, enhances customer service, and personalizes shopping experiences, leading to increased efficiency and customer satisfaction.

Furthermore, ML has a significant impact on the field of natural language processing, enabling machines to understand and interpret human language with increasing accuracy, thus bridging the communication gap between humans and technology. This advancement has led to the development of sophisticated virtual assistants and has revolutionized the way we interact with devices and access information.

The applications of machine learning also extend to more critical areas like environmental conservation and climate change, where ML algorithms analyze vast amounts of environmental data to track changes, predict trends, and propose solutions. In the realm of education, adaptive learning systems personalize the educational experience, catering to the unique needs of each student and revolutionizing the traditional learning process.

Each application of ML brings with it a set of challenges, opportunities, and ethical considerations, underscoring the need for responsible use of this technology. As we delve into the myriad applications of machine learning in this section, we gain not only an appreciation for the versatility and power of ML but also an understanding of the responsibilities that come with its deployment. The transformative potential of ML is immense, and its applications are only limited by our imagination and the ethical boundaries we set as a society.

4.1 Exploration of Various Industries and Their ML Applications

The application of machine learning across various industries marks a significant leap in how technology is leveraged to enhance efficiency, accuracy, and innovation. In this section, we embark on a detailed journey to uncover how ML is revolutionizing different sectors, from healthcare and retail to finance and banking. This exploration sheds light on the transformative impact of ML, showcasing its versatility and capability to adapt to the unique challenges and needs of each industry. As we delve into the specific applications in each sector, we gain insights into the profound ways in which ML is reshaping industry landscapes and driving progress.

4.1.1 ML in Healthcare: Revolutionizing Diagnosis and Treatment

Healthcare is one of the sectors where ML's impact is most profound. ML technologies in healthcare are revolutionizing patient diagnosis, treatment, and care in several ways:

Predictive Analytics: ML algorithms analyze patient data to predict health risks and outcomes, enabling preventative care and early interventions.

Medical Imaging: Advanced ML models, particularly those based on deep learning, are being used to interpret medical images like X-rays and MRIs with greater accuracy and speed, aiding in the diagnosis of diseases.

Personalized Medicine: ML facilitates the analysis of large datasets to tailor treatment plans to individual patients, improving the efficacy of treatments.

Drug Discovery and Development: ML speeds up the process of drug discovery by predicting the potential efficacy and side effects of new drugs.

4.1.2 Transforming Retail and Ecommerce with ML

In retail and ecommerce, ML is transforming the shopping experience, supply chain management, and marketing strategies:

Personalized Customer Experiences: ML algorithms analyze customer data to provide personalized product recommendations, enhancing the shopping experience.

Inventory Management: ML helps in predicting demand, optimizing stock levels, and thereby reducing costs and improving efficiency.

Price Optimization: ML models can dynamically adjust prices based on factors like demand, competition, and market conditions.

4.1.3 The Role of ML in Financial Services and Banking

ML is playing a crucial role in reshaping the financial services and banking industry:

Fraud Detection: ML algorithms are adept at detecting patterns indicative of fraudulent activities, thereby enhancing the security of financial transactions.

Risk Management: ML models assess credit risk, market risk, and operational risk by analyzing vast amounts of data to make informed decisions.

Algorithmic Trading: In financial markets, ML algorithms are used to develop trading strategies that can adapt to market changes in real-time.

Customer Service: Chatbots and virtual assistants powered by ML provide efficient customer service, reducing the need for human intervention.

The exploration of ML applications across various industries reveals its significant and growing influence. In healthcare, it is paving the way for more accurate diagnoses and personalized treatment. In retail and ecommerce, it is optimizing operations and enhancing customer experiences. In the realm of finance and banking, it is improving security and enabling smarter decision-making. Machine learning's ability to process and analyze vast amounts of data makes it an invaluable asset across these diverse sectors, driving innovation and efficiency.

4.2 Case Studies of Successful ML Implementations

Machine learning is not just a theoretical concept; its real-world implementations have led to groundbreaking innovations across various domains. This section offers a detailed examination of how ML has been applied to create tangible and impactful solutions in different sectors. This section delves into three key areas where ML has made significant strides: autonomous vehicles, AI-powered personal assistants, and predictive analytics in business intelligence. These case studies not only showcase the practical applications of ML but also highlight the transformative impact of this technology in solving complex challenges and creating new possibilities.

4.2.1 Innovations in Autonomous Vehicles: A ML Perspective

One of the most exciting applications of ML is in the development of autonomous vehicles. These self-driving cars and trucks use ML algorithms to interpret sensor data, enabling them to understand their surroundings and make real-time decisions. Key innovations include:

Sensor Fusion: ML algorithms integrate data from various sensors like cameras, radars, and Lidar to create a comprehensive understanding of the vehicle's environment.

Object Detection and Classification: ML models identify and classify objects around the vehicle, distinguishing between other vehicles, pedestrians, traffic signs, and more.

Path Planning and Decision Making: ML enables vehicles to plan their paths, make decisions at intersections, change lanes, and adjust to unexpected situations like roadblocks or erratic drivers.

Companies like Tesla, Waymo, and others have made significant progress in this field, moving closer to fully autonomous driving.

4.2.2 AI-Powered Personal Assistants: A Success Story

AI-powered personal assistants like Siri, Alexa, and Google Assistant are prime examples of ML's success. These assistants use natural language processing, a branch of ML, to understand and respond to user commands. Key aspects include:

Voice Recognition: Advanced ML models accurately convert spoken words into text, understanding different accents and dialects.

Contextual Understanding: These assistants use ML to understand the context of queries, providing more accurate and relevant responses.

Personalization: ML algorithms learn from individual user interactions to personalize responses and anticipate needs.

The widespread adoption of these assistants in smartphones and smart home devices highlights the practicality and user-friendliness of ML technologies.

4.2.3 Breakthroughs in Predictive Analytics for Business Intelligence

Predictive analytics in business intelligence is another area where ML has shown remarkable results. Companies across various industries use ML to analyze data and predict future trends, which helps in making informed business decisions. Key applications include:

Customer Behavior Prediction: ML models analyze customer data to predict purchasing patterns, helping businesses tailor their marketing strategies.

Supply Chain Optimization: ML algorithms forecast demand and supply needs, optimizing inventory management and reducing costs.

Risk Management: Financial institutions use ML to assess credit risk and detect potential fraudulent transactions.

These case studies illustrate the diverse and impactful applications of machine learning, demonstrating its capability to drive innovation and efficiency. From enhancing safety in autonomous vehicles to improving user experience with personal assistants, and enabling smarter business decisions through predictive analytics, ML implementations are setting new benchmarks in technological advancements.

4.3 ROI and Impact Assessment of ML Projects

Assessing the return on investment (ROI) and the broader impact of machine learning projects is crucial for understanding their value and guiding future initiatives. This section explores the multifaceted aspects of evaluating the effectiveness and influence of ML initiatives. This section provides an in-depth look at the methodologies for measuring the success of ML projects, the long-term impacts of ML on business performance, and how ML-driven insights can inform strategic decision-making. As ML continues to embed itself in various business processes, its ROI and impact become vital metrics for organizations looking to invest in this technology.

4.3.1 Measuring Success: Evaluating ROI in ML Projects

Determining the ROI of ML projects involves several key considerations:

Cost-Benefit Analysis: This involves comparing the costs associated with developing and deploying the ML project, including computational resources, data acquisition, and personnel, against the benefits gained, such as increased efficiency, revenue growth, or cost savings.

Performance Metrics: Evaluating the performance improvements brought about by the ML system, such as accuracy, speed, and scalability, is essential. These metrics should align with the project's initial goals and objectives.

Market Impact: Assessing how the ML project has affected the organization's market position, such as increased market share or enhanced customer satisfaction, can provide insight into its broader business impact.

4.3.2 Long-Term Impacts of ML on Business Performance

The long-term impacts of ML on business are profound and multifaceted:

Operational Efficiency: ML can automate routine tasks, streamline operations, and optimize processes, leading to long-term operational efficiency and cost savings.

Competitive Advantage: By harnessing data-driven insights, businesses can gain a competitive edge, whether through improved customer experiences, personalized services, or innovative products.

Organizational Transformation: ML can act as a catalyst for broader digital transformation, encouraging data-driven cultures and informed decision-making across the organization.

4.3.3 Strategic Decision Making Driven by ML Insights

ML insights play a significant role in shaping strategic decisions:

Data-Driven Strategies: ML enables organizations to base their strategies on comprehensive data analysis, leading to more informed and effective decision-making.

Risk Management: ML tools can identify and assess potential risks, allowing businesses to develop strategies to mitigate these risks proactively.

Innovation and Development: Insights from ML projects can highlight new opportunities for innovation, guiding research and development efforts towards areas with the highest potential impact.

Evaluating the ROI and impact of ML projects is a complex but essential process. It requires a comprehensive assessment of both tangible and intangible factors. By effectively measuring the success and long-term impacts of ML initiatives, organizations can not only justify their investments but also refine their strategies and operations for continuous improvement and growth in an increasingly data-driven world.

Chapter 5: In-depth Exploration of Machine Learning Algorithms

The heart of machine learning's transformative power lies in its algorithms - the intricate set of rules and statistical processes that teach machines to make sense of and act upon data. This chapter presents a comprehensive journey into the core of machine learning, unraveling the complexities and nuances of various algorithms that constitute the backbone of this field. This chapter is an odyssey into the diverse landscape of algorithms, each uniquely designed to interpret data, draw insights, and make decisions.

From foundational algorithms that have been the pillars of the field to cutting-edge techniques pushing the boundaries of what machines can learn and achieve, this chapter offers a detailed analysis of each category. Understanding these algorithms is crucial, as they are the tools that translate raw data into actionable intelligence. They are the unseen engines driving advancements in numerous sectors, including healthcare, finance, transportation, and more.

The exploration begins with supervised learning algorithms, where machines learn from labeled data, understanding the relationship between input and output. It then transitions into the realm of unsupervised learning, where algorithms discern patterns and structures in unlabeled data. The journey also encompasses semi-supervised and reinforcement learning, where algorithms learn with limited data or through interaction with an environment.

Each section of this chapter not only breaks down the theoretical underpinnings of these algorithms but also provides insights into their practical applications, strengths, and limitations. The discussions extend to advanced topics like deep learning, where neural networks, inspired by the human brain, process complex data inputs. These discussions are complemented by real-world examples and case studies, illustrating how these algorithms are applied to solve specific problems.

The chapter also addresses the challenges in algorithm implementation, such as overfitting, underfitting, and the need for data preprocessing. It delves into the trade-offs between different algorithms, guiding readers on how to select the most appropriate technique for a given problem.

This chapter is designed to equip readers - from aspiring data scientists to seasoned AI professionals - with a deep understanding of how various machine learning algorithms work, how they are evolving, and how they can be harnessed to unlock the full potential of data-driven solutions. This comprehensive overview not only serves as a guide to the current landscape of machine learning algorithms but also offers a glimpse into the future trajectory of this rapidly evolving field.

5.1 Detailed Discussion of Different ML Algorithms

Machine learning is a field rich with various algorithms, each designed to tackle specific types of problems and data. This chapter is an extensive exploration into the world of ML algorithms, shedding light on the intricacies and nuances that define their functionality and applicability. This section is structured to provide a thorough understanding of the primary categories of ML algorithms: supervised, unsupervised, and reinforcement learning. It also delves into the subcategories of classification, regression, and clustering algorithms, and offers an insight into the sophisticated realm of deep learning, from basic neural networks to more advanced architectures. This discussion is not just about theoretical knowledge; it also touches upon practical applications, providing a comprehensive perspective on how these algorithms function in real-world scenarios.

5.1.1 Overview of Supervised, Unsupervised, and Reinforcement Learning Algorithms

Supervised Learning: This category involves algorithms that learn from labeled training data, aiming to make predictions or decisions. Common supervised learning algorithms include linear regression for continuous output prediction and logistic regression, support vector machines (SVM), and decision trees for classification tasks.

Unsupervised Learning: In unsupervised learning, algorithms deal with unlabeled data. Their goal is to find underlying patterns or groupings in the data. Key techniques include clustering methods like k-means, hierarchical clustering, and dimensionality reduction techniques like principal component analysis (PCA).

Reinforcement Learning: Reinforcement learning algorithms learn to make decisions by performing actions in an environment to achieve a goal. They learn from the outcomes of their actions, rather than from being taught explicitly. This category includes algorithms like Q-learning and policy gradient methods.

5.1.2 Breaking Down Classification, Regression, and Clustering Algorithms

Classification Algorithms: These are used for predictive modeling problems where the output variable is a category, such as "spam" or "not spam." Examples include Naïve Bayes, k-Nearest Neighbors (k-NN), and Random Forests.

Regression Algorithms: Used when the output is a real or continuous value, such as "house price" or "temperature." Linear regression and polynomial regression are common examples, alongside more complex methods like ridge and lasso regression.

Clustering Algorithms: These algorithms group a set of objects in such a way that objects in the same group are more similar to each other than to those in other groups. Examples include k-means clustering, DBSCAN, and Gaussian mixture models.

5.1.3 Deep Learning Algorithms: From Neural Networks to Advanced Architectures

Neural Networks: The basic building blocks of deep learning, neural networks, consist of neurons with learnable weights and biases. They are used for a wide range of applications, from simple tasks like linear regression to complex functions like image and speech recognition.

Convolutional Neural Networks (CNNs): Especially effective for image processing, CNNs include layers that automatically and adaptively learn spatial hierarchies of features from input images.

Recurrent Neural Networks (RNNs) and Long Short-Term Memory (LSTM): Ideal for sequential data such as time series or natural language, these algorithms can remember information for long periods, which is essential in understanding context in text or predicting the next moment in time series data.

Advanced Architectures: This includes newer architectures like Transformers, which have been revolutionary in natural language processing tasks, and Generative Adversarial Networks (GANs), which are used for generating new data that resembles the given input data.

Understanding the different types of ML algorithms and their applications is crucial for anyone looking to apply ML in real-world scenarios. Each algorithm has its strengths and is suited for specific types of problems and data. This detailed overview provides a solid foundation for exploring the vast and dynamic world of machine learning algorithms.

5.2 When and How to Use Specific ML Algorithms

Navigating the world of machine learning involves not just understanding different algorithms but also knowing when and how to apply them effectively. This section is a critical exploration into the art of selecting the most appropriate ML techniques for various scenarios. This section provides guidance on how to match ML algorithms to specific data types and problems, discusses the advantages and limitations of different algorithmic approaches, and considers the impact of data size and complexity on algorithm selection. This knowledge is essential for ML practitioners to make informed decisions that lead to successful outcomes in their ML projects.

5.2.1 Selecting the Right Algorithm for Your Data and Problem

The selection of an ML algorithm depends largely on the nature of the problem and the type of data at hand:

Nature of the Problem: Identify whether the problem is a classification, regression, clustering, or another type of task. For example, use classification algorithms like decision trees or support vector machines for categorical output, and regression algorithms like linear regression for continuous output.

Type of Data: Consider the data's characteristics is it labeled or unlabeled, structured or unstructured? For instance, neural networks are well-suited for complex data like images and audio, while simpler algorithms like logistic regression might be more appropriate for structured, tabular data.

5.2.2 Pros and Cons of Different Algorithmic Approaches

Each ML algorithm comes with its set of strengths and weaknesses:

Ease of Interpretation vs. Model Complexity: Simpler models like decision trees are easy to interpret but might not capture complex relationships as well as more complex models like neural networks.

Training Time: Some algorithms, particularly deep learning models, require significant computational resources and time to train, while others like Naive Bayes are much faster.

Accuracy vs. Overfitting: Highly accurate models may risk overfitting, particularly in cases where the data is not sufficiently diverse, or the model is too complex for the task.

5.2.3 Algorithm Selection in the Context of Data Size and Complexity

The size and complexity of the dataset play a crucial role in algorithm selection:

Large Datasets: More complex models like deep learning algorithms can perform better with large datasets as they have the capacity to learn from a vast amount of data.

Small Datasets: For smaller datasets, simpler models or techniques like k-nearest neighbors or support vector machines might be more effective to avoid overfitting.

High-Dimensional Data: When dealing with high-dimensional data, dimensionality reduction techniques can be applied before using ML algorithms to simplify the data without losing critical information.

The selection of ML algorithms is a nuanced process that depends on various factors, including the nature of the problem, the type and size of the data, and the specific requirements of the task. Understanding these factors and the characteristics of different algorithms is key to choosing the most effective technique for any given ML project. This section provides essential insights and considerations that guide practitioners in making strategic decisions about algorithm selection, thereby enhancing the effectiveness and efficiency of their ML solutions.

5.3 Practical Examples and Case Studies

The true test of machine learning algorithms lies in their application to real-world scenarios. This section offers a vivid showcase of how ML algorithms are applied across various industries, demonstrating their transformative power and versatility. This section delves into a range of real-world applications, celebrates notable success stories, and extracts valuable lessons from the challenges encountered during the implementation of ML algorithms. By examining these practical examples and case studies, we gain not only a deeper appreciation for the potential of ML but also an understanding of the practical considerations and strategic approaches necessary for successful implementation.

5.3.1 Real-World Applications of ML Algorithms in Various Industries

ML algorithms find diverse applications across various sectors, each with its unique challenges and objectives:

Healthcare: ML algorithms are used for predictive diagnostics, personalized medicine, and medical image analysis. For example, deep learning models analyze X-ray images to detect anomalies like tumors or fractures.

Finance: In finance, ML algorithms are deployed for fraud detection, credit scoring, and algorithmic trading. Predictive models analyze transaction patterns to identify potential fraud, enhancing security measures.

Retail: ML powers recommendation systems, customer segmentation, and inventory management in retail. Algorithms analyze customer data to personalize shopping experiences and predict product demand.

Manufacturing: In manufacturing, ML enhances quality control, predictive maintenance, and supply chain optimization. Predictive models forecast equipment failures, reducing downtime and maintenance costs.

5.3.2 Case Studies: Success Stories in Machine Learning

Some of the most impactful success stories in ML demonstrate the technology's capacity to solve complex problems:

Autonomous Vehicles: Companies like Tesla and Waymo have made significant strides in developing self-driving cars using ML algorithms that process data from sensors to navigate roads safely.

Language Translation Services: Services like Google Translate use neural networks for real-time language translation, breaking down language barriers globally.

E-commerce Personalization: Amazon's recommendation system is a prime example of ML's application in personalizing user experiences, significantly boosting sales and customer satisfaction.

5.3.3 Lessons Learned: Challenges and Solutions in Implementing ML Algorithms

Implementing ML algorithms comes with its set of challenges, from which valuable lessons can be drawn:

Data Quality and Quantity: One of the biggest challenges is ensuring high-quality, sufficient data for training models. Overcoming this often requires meticulous data collection and preprocessing.

Balancing Accuracy and Complexity: Achieving high accuracy without overcomplicating the model is a common challenge. Solutions involve model tuning and validation techniques to strike the right balance.

Ethical and Privacy Considerations: Addressing ethical concerns and ensuring data privacy are crucial. This involves implementing robust data governance policies and ethical guidelines in ML development.

The practical examples and case studies in this section provide a panoramic view of ML's applications, successes, and challenges. These real-world scenarios not only illustrate the potential and adaptability of ML algorithms across different industries but also offer insights into overcoming the hurdles encountered in their implementation. This comprehensive overview serves as both an inspiration and a guide for those seeking to leverage ML to address complex problems and innovate within their fields.

Chapter 6: Exploring Open-Source Libraries in Machine Learning

In the dynamic and ever-evolving field of machine learning, open-source libraries stand as pillars of innovation and collaboration. This chapter offers an in-depth look at the wealth of resources available in the open-source community, showcasing how these libraries not only democratize access to advanced ML technologies but also foster a culture of knowledge sharing and collective problem-solving. This exploration dives into the diverse range of open-source libraries available, each offering unique functionalities, algorithms, and tools suited to different aspects of ML.

Open-source libraries in ML are a testament to the power of collaborative development, enabling individuals and organizations worldwide to access cutting-edge technology without prohibitive costs. These libraries serve as the foundation for a multitude of ML applications, from academic research to industry-scale projects. They provide the building blocks for developing sophisticated ML models, including data preprocessing, algorithm implementation, model training, and evaluation.

This section begins by detailing the most popular and widely used open-source libraries such as TensorFlow, PyTorch, Scikit-learn, and Keras. Each library is examined for its specific strengths, use cases, and the unique ecosystem it offers to ML practitioners. TensorFlow and PyTorch, for instance, are renowned for their powerful deep learning capabilities and flexible architectures, making them favorites in both research and industry settings. Scikit-learn, with its user-friendly interface and extensive range of algorithms for classical ML tasks, is often the go-to choice for beginners and experts looking to implement traditional ML models efficiently.

Moreover, the exploration delves into specialized libraries that cater to specific ML domains, such as NLP, computer vision, and time-series analysis. Libraries like NLTK and spaCy offer tools and functionalities tailored for processing and understanding human language, while OpenCV specializes in image and video analysis.

The section also discusses the importance of community support and documentation that accompany these open-source libraries, highlighting how they contribute to the ease of learning and implementation. It covers how the open-source nature of these libraries not only facilitates accessibility and innovation but also ensures transparency and reliability, crucial aspects in the field of ML.

This chapter is designed to guide readers through the rich landscape of available tools, helping them to select and utilize the appropriate libraries for their ML projects. This comprehensive overview not only highlights the practical aspects of these libraries but also emphasizes the spirit of open source – a collaborative, inclusive, and continually advancing journey in the quest for knowledge and innovation in machine learning.

6.1 Overview of Popular Open-Source ML Libraries

The landscape of machine learning is richly adorned with a variety of open-source libraries, each offering distinct capabilities and tools that have significantly contributed to the growth and accessibility of ML technologies. In this chapter, we embark on a comprehensive survey of these libraries, uncovering their unique features, functionalities, and the roles they play in the advancement of ML. This exploration is not just about listing these tools but understanding their essence – how they have evolved, what trends they are setting in the ML community, and the specific needs they address. From the general-purpose libraries that have become synonymous with ML to the specialized ones catering to niche areas, this section offers a panoramic view of the open-source tools at the disposal of ML practitioners.

6.1.1 Survey of Leading ML Libraries and Their Capabilities

Several open-source libraries have risen to prominence in the ML community, each known for its specific strengths:

TensorFlow: Developed by Google, TensorFlow is renowned for its powerful computation capabilities, especially in deep learning. It offers a flexible architecture and is widely used in research and production alike.

PyTorch: Created by Facebook's AI Research lab, PyTorch is praised for its user-friendly interface and dynamic computation graph, making it a favorite for research and prototyping.

Scikit-learn: Known for its simplicity and accessibility, Scikit-learn is a go-to library for classical ML algorithms, providing tools for data preprocessing, classification, regression, clustering, and more.

Keras: Keras, now integrated with TensorFlow, stands out for its high-level neural networks API, designed for human readability and ease of use, making it suitable for beginners.

6.1.2 Evolution and Development Trends in Open-Source ML Libraries

The evolution of these libraries reflects broader trends in the ML field:

From Static to Dynamic: There's a shift towards dynamic computation graphs, as seen in PyTorch, which allows for more intuitive coding of complex models.

Scalability and Performance: Libraries are continuously being optimized for performance and scalability to handle large datasets and complex neural networks.

Integration and Standardization: Greater emphasis is being placed on integration and interoperability between libraries, as seen in the TensorFlow-Keras integration.

6.1.3 Key Features and Functionalities of Prominent ML Libraries

Each library brings a set of key features and functionalities:

TensorFlow: Offers robust distributed training capabilities, a vast array of tools for various tasks like TensorFlow Lite for mobile, and TensorBoard for visualization.

PyTorch: Provides excellent support for GPU acceleration and is known for its flexibility, ease of debugging, and a strong community for research.

Scikit-learn: Its appeal lies in its broad array of algorithms accessible through a consistent interface, making it ideal for educational purposes and small to medium-scale applications.

Keras: Enables fast experimentation with deep neural networks, providing a modular and extensible architecture.

The realm of open-source ML libraries is dynamic and diverse. Each library's evolution, key features, and functionalities represent the cutting edge of ML technology, offering tools that cater to a wide range of applications and requirements. Understanding these libraries is crucial for anyone venturing into the ML field, as they provide the foundational tools and frameworks required to turn ML concepts into practical applications.

6.2 Comparative Analysis and Use Case Recommendations

As the field of machine learning continues to expand, so does the diversity of open-source libraries available, each offering unique strengths and capabilities. This section provides a detailed evaluation and comparison of these ML libraries, guiding users in selecting the most appropriate tool for their specific project needs. This section not only compares the features and functionalities of various ML libraries but also aligns them with different types of ML projects, offering practical insights into their optimal use. Through case studies, we explore real-world scenarios where these libraries have been effectively utilized, showcasing their application in diverse contexts and projects.

6.2.1 Evaluating and Comparing Different ML Libraries

A critical aspect of selecting an ML library is understanding how each library performs under different conditions and requirements:

Performance and Scalability: Libraries like TensorFlow and PyTorch are known for their high performance and scalability, particularly in handling large datasets and complex deep learning models.

Ease of Use and Flexibility: For beginners or projects that require rapid prototyping, libraries such as Scikit-learn and Keras are more user-friendly and offer greater flexibility.

Support for Specific ML Tasks: Some libraries are tailored for specific tasks, like NLTK or spaCy for natural language processing, and OpenCV for computer vision.

Community and Ecosystem: The size and activity of a library's community can be crucial for support, troubleshooting, and staying updated with the latest advancements.

6.2.2 Matching ML Libraries to Specific Project Needs

Selecting the right ML library often depends on the specific requirements and objectives of a project:

Nature of the ML Task: For deep learning tasks, TensorFlow or PyTorch might be preferred. For more traditional ML tasks like classification or regression, Scikit-learn could be more suitable.

Project Size and Complexity: Larger, more complex projects might benefit from the robustness of TensorFlow, while smaller projects might find the simplicity of Scikit-learn more appropriate.

Development Timeframe: Projects with tight deadlines might prioritize libraries with easier learning curves and faster implementation, like Keras.

6.2.3 Case Studies: Effective Use of ML Libraries in Diverse Scenarios

Various case studies illustrate the effective application of these libraries in real-world scenarios:

TensorFlow in Image Recognition: TensorFlow has been successfully used in complex image recognition tasks, leveraging its advanced deep learning capabilities.

Scikit-learn in Customer Segmentation: Scikit-learn, with its array of clustering algorithms, has been effectively used in market segmentation and customer analysis projects.

PyTorch in Academic Research: PyTorch, known for its dynamic computation graph and ease of use, is widely used in academic research for experimenting with novel deep learning models.

The comparative analysis and use case recommendations for ML libraries provide a roadmap for practitioners to navigate the broad spectrum of tools available in the ML landscape. Understanding the strengths, weaknesses, and best application scenarios for each library allows for more informed decision-making and ultimately leads to more successful and efficient ML projects.

6.3 Integration of Libraries into ML Workflows

The effective integration of machine learning libraries into workflows is a key factor in the success of ML projects. This section delves into the strategic incorporation of these powerful tools into various stages of ML projects, from data preprocessing to model deployment. This section explores the best practices for embedding ML libraries into workflows, addresses the challenges commonly faced during integration, and highlights how the unique features and tools of these libraries can enhance ML processes. Proper integration not only streamlines the workflow but also maximizes the efficiency and effectiveness of ML projects.

6.3.1 Best Practices for Incorporating ML Libraries into Projects

Incorporating ML libraries into projects requires a thoughtful approach that aligns with the project's goals:

Understanding Library Strengths: Begin by understanding the strengths and limitations of each library. Match the library's capabilities with the project's needs to ensure it can effectively address the specific challenges of the task.

Maintaining Workflow Consistency: Integrate the library in a way that maintains consistency in the ML workflow. This involves ensuring that data formats, preprocessing methods, and model outputs are compatible across different stages of the workflow.

Modular Integration: Adopt a modular approach to integration, where the ML library can be easily replaced or updated without disrupting the entire workflow. This flexibility is crucial for adapting to new developments in ML technologies.

6.3.2 Overcoming Challenges in Library Integration

Integrating ML libraries into workflows can present several challenges:

Compatibility Issues: One common challenge is ensuring compatibility between the library and existing systems or other libraries. This may require adjustments in data formats or processing methods.

Performance Optimization: Optimize the performance of the integrated library, particularly in terms of processing speed and resource usage, to ensure it does not become a bottleneck in the workflow.

Staying Updated: Keep abreast of updates and changes to the libraries, as new versions may introduce enhancements or changes that could impact the workflow.

6.3.3 Enhancing ML Workflows with Library Features and Tools

ML libraries offer a range of features and tools that can significantly enhance ML workflows:

Automated Data Preprocessing: Many libraries provide tools for automated data cleaning, normalization, and feature extraction, which can save time and improve model performance.

Advanced Model Training Features: Utilize advanced features like hyperparameter tuning, cross-validation, and GPU acceleration for efficient model training.

Visualization and Analysis Tools: Leverage built-in tools for data visualization and model analysis to gain insights and improve model accuracy.

Deployment Tools: Some libraries offer tools for easy model deployment, enabling seamless transition from the development stage to production.

The integration of ML libraries into workflows is a critical aspect of ML project development. By following best practices, addressing challenges effectively, and leveraging the unique features of these libraries, ML practitioners can enhance the efficiency and effectiveness of their ML workflows. This integration is key to harnessing the full potential of ML libraries, ultimately leading to more successful and impactful ML projects.

Chapter 7: Data Engineering and Training Data for Machine Learning

In the intricate and multifaceted world of machine learning, data engineering and the quality of training data form the cornerstone of successful model development. This chapter provides a deep dive into the critical processes and methodologies involved in preparing and managing data, a phase that significantly influences the effectiveness of ML models. This exploration acknowledges that data is not merely a raw material for ML; it's the lifeblood that fuels algorithms, guiding their learning processes and shaping their outputs.

The journey through this section begins with the understanding that data engineering is an art and a science, requiring a meticulous approach to collecting, processing, transforming, and managing data. It involves creating robust data pipelines that ensure the seamless flow of high-quality data through various stages of an ML project. The section underscores the importance of training data, which is foundational in teaching ML models how to make predictions or take actions. The quality, diversity, and representativeness of training data directly impact a model's ability to learn effectively and generalize to new, unseen data.

Further, we delve into the nuances of data preprocessing – an often underappreciated yet crucial step in ML. This includes techniques for data cleaning, normalization, feature extraction, and dimensionality reduction, all of which are essential for transforming raw data into a format that is suitable for ML models. The section also explores the challenges associated with data engineering, such as handling missing or imbalanced data, dealing with noisy or unstructured data, and ensuring data privacy and security.

The discussion extends to cover advanced topics in data engineering, such as the use of big data technologies, cloud-based data storage and processing, and automated data pipelines. These technologies and practices not only enhance the efficiency of data handling but also scale up the capabilities of ML systems to deal with increasingly large and complex datasets.

This chapter aims to equip readers with a comprehensive understanding of the vital role that data engineering plays in the ML lifecycle. It provides insights into best practices, challenges, and solutions in handling training data, emphasizing that effective data engineering is a prerequisite for building robust and accurate ML models. This section is an invaluable resource for anyone involved in ML, from data scientists and engineers to ML practitioners and enthusiasts, highlighting that in the realm of machine learning, quality data engineering is just as crucial as sophisticated algorithms.

7.1 Strategies for Data Collection and Management

In the world of machine learning, effective data collection and management are as crucial as the algorithms themselves. This section delves into the methodologies and practices essential for handling one of the most critical assets in ML: data. This section outlines best practices for collecting data efficiently, techniques for managing large datasets, and strategies for storing and retrieving data. Understanding these strategies is fundamental for ML practitioners, as the quality and accessibility of data directly impact the performance and success of ML models.

7.1.1 Best Practices for Efficient Data Collection

Efficient data collection is the first step in building a strong foundation for ML models:

Define Clear Objectives: Begin by clearly defining what data is needed, based on the objectives of the ML project. This helps in collecting data that is relevant and valuable.

Diverse and Representative Data: Ensure the data collected is diverse and representative of the real-world scenario the model will be applied to. This prevents biases and improves the model's generalizability.

Automate Data Collection: Where possible, automate the data collection process using APIs, web scraping, or sensors. Automation increases efficiency and reduces the likelihood of human error.

Data Privacy and Ethics: Always consider privacy and ethical implications while collecting data. Ensure compliance with data protection regulations and obtain necessary consents.

7.1.2 Managing Large Datasets for Machine Learning

Handling large datasets requires strategic approaches to ensure scalability and efficiency:

Data Partitioning and Sampling: For extremely large datasets, partitioning the data and using sampling techniques can make the dataset more manageable.

Use of Big Data Technologies: Implement big data technologies like Hadoop or Spark for distributed data processing and storage. These technologies are designed to handle vast amounts of data efficiently.

Data Cleaning and Preprocessing: Regularly clean and preprocess the data to maintain its quality. This includes handling missing values, removing duplicates, and normalizing data.

7.1.3 Data Storage and Retrieval Strategies in ML

Effective data storage and retrieval are key to ensuring data is accessible and usable for ML:

Scalable Storage Solutions: Utilize scalable storage solutions like cloud storage (AWS S3, Google Cloud Storage) that can grow with your data needs.

Database Management: Choose the appropriate type of database (SQL or NoSQL) based on the structure and requirements of your data.

Efficient Data Retrieval: Implement efficient data retrieval practices, such as indexing and query optimization, to reduce the time taken to access data.

Data Versioning: Keep track of different versions of datasets, especially in dynamic environments where data is constantly updated. This helps in maintaining consistency and reproducibility in ML models.

The strategies for data collection and management are critical in the realm of ML. By adhering to best practices in data collection, effectively managing large datasets, and employing robust data storage and retrieval strategies, ML practitioners can ensure that their models are built on a foundation of high-quality, relevant, and accessible data. These practices not only enhance the performance of ML models but also contribute to their scalability and reliability in various applications.

7.2 Preprocessing and Cleaning Training Data

The preprocessing and cleaning of training data are pivotal steps in the machine learning pipeline, often determining the success or failure of ML models. This section dives into the essential techniques and practices that transform raw data into a refined format ready for ML algorithms. This section breaks down the process of data preprocessing, discusses how to identify and address data anomalies, and explores the automation of data cleansing processes. Given that ML models are only as good as the data they learn from, this stage is crucial in ensuring the integrity and quality of the input data.

7.2.1 Techniques for Effective Data Preprocessing

Effective data preprocessing involves several key techniques:

Normalization and Standardization: Adjusting the scale of features to a standard range improves model training efficiency and accuracy. Techniques like Min-Max scaling and Z-score normalization are commonly used.

Encoding Categorical Data: Convert categorical data into a format that can be easily interpreted by ML algorithms. Techniques include one-hot encoding and label encoding.

Handling Missing Values: Strategies for dealing with missing data include imputation (filling missing values with statistical measures like mean or median) or removing rows/columns with missing values.

Feature Engineering: Extract and select the most relevant features from the data to improve model performance. This includes creating new features that better capture the underlying patterns in the data.

7.2.2 Identifying and Addressing Data Anomalies

Data anomalies can significantly skew the results of an ML model:

Outlier Detection: Identify and address outliers data points that significantly differ from other observations. Methods include statistical techniques like IQR (Interquartile Range) or visual methods like box plots.

Error Correction: Correct data entry errors or inconsistencies. This can be achieved through rule-based approaches or anomaly detection algorithms.

Data Validation: Implement validation rules to ensure data accuracy and consistency, particularly for new data entering the system.

7.2.3 Automating Data Cleansing Processes

Automating the data cleansing process can save time and increase efficiency:

Data Cleansing Tools: Utilize data cleansing tools and software that offer automated features for detecting and correcting anomalies in data.

Machine Learning Models for Data Cleansing: Implement ML models specifically designed to detect and correct errors in datasets.

Continuous Monitoring: Set up systems for continuous monitoring of data quality, with automated alerts and actions for potential issues.

Preprocessing and cleaning training data are critical steps in the ML process, directly impacting the model's performance. By effectively employing techniques for data normalization, encoding, handling missing values, and feature engineering, practitioners can significantly improve their model's accuracy and reliability. Furthermore, identifying and addressing data anomalies and automating the data cleansing process are key to maintaining the quality and integrity of the data over time. These steps ensure that the foundation upon which ML models are built is solid and reliable, setting the stage for successful ML outcomes.

7.3 Ensuring Data Quality and Integrity

Data quality and integrity are fundamental to the success of machine learning projects. This section addresses the critical aspect of maintaining the accuracy and consistency of data throughout the ML process. This section explores the strategies and measures necessary to uphold high data quality, examines the challenges related to data integrity in ML projects, and discusses the implementation of data validation techniques. Ensuring data quality and integrity is crucial, as even the most sophisticated ML models can yield poor results if the underlying data is flawed or unreliable.

7.3.1 Measures to Maintain High Data Quality

Maintaining high data quality involves several key measures:

Regular Audits: Conduct regular audits of the data to identify and rectify quality issues like inaccuracies, inconsistencies, and duplicates.

Robust Data Collection Procedures: Establish robust procedures for data collection to ensure that the data is accurate and reliable from the outset.

Data Cleaning: Implement thorough data cleaning processes, including the removal of outliers, correction of errors, and handling of missing values.

Data Updating: Keep the data updated to reflect the most current information, which is especially important in dynamic environments where data changes frequently.

7.3.2 Data Integrity Challenges in ML Projects

Data integrity in ML projects can be challenged in various ways:

Data Drift: This occurs when the statistical properties of the input data change over time, potentially reducing the model's accuracy.

Scalability Issues: As data volume grows, maintaining the quality and consistency of the data can become increasingly challenging.

Integration of Diverse Data Sources: Combining data from various sources can introduce inconsistencies and quality issues.

7.3.3 Implementing Data Validation Techniques

Data validation is essential to ensure the integrity and quality of the data used in ML models:

Validation Rules: Establish rules for data validation to identify anomalies, outliers, and patterns that do not conform to expected standards.

Automated Validation Tools: Utilize automated tools for continuous monitoring and validation of data quality. These tools can quickly identify and alert about potential issues.

Cross-Validation with Multiple Data Sources: Where possible, cross-validate the data with multiple sources to ensure its accuracy and reliability.

Ensuring data quality and integrity is a critical component of successful ML projects. By implementing rigorous measures to maintain high data quality, addressing challenges related to data integrity, and employing robust data validation techniques, practitioners can ensure that their ML models are built on a foundation of reliable and accurate data. This focus on data quality and integrity not only enhances the performance of ML models but also contributes to their credibility and trustworthiness in real-world applications.

Chapter 8: Feature Engineering, Model Development, and Model Deployment

In the multifaceted world of machine learning, the journey from raw data to a fully functional ML model involves several critical stages: feature engineering, model development, and model deployment. Each of these stages is an integral part of the ML pipeline, playing a unique and pivotal role in transforming theoretical concepts into practical, real-world applications. This chapter delves into these essential components, providing a comprehensive guide through the processes that form the backbone of any successful ML project.

Feature Engineering is the art and science of selecting, manipulating, and transforming raw data into features that better represent the underlying problem to predictive models, thereby improving their accuracy and performance. This stage is where domain knowledge, creativity, and technical skills converge to extract and craft the most relevant and informative attributes from datasets.

Model Development is the core phase where algorithms come into play. It involves selecting appropriate ML models, tuning hyperparameters, and training the models with prepared datasets. This phase requires a deep understanding of both the data at hand and the range of available ML algorithms, as well as the skill to match the two effectively.

Model Deployment marks the transition of ML models from a development environment to a production setting where they can provide predictions on new data. This stage is crucial as it involves not just the technical deployment of the model but also considerations regarding scalability, maintainability, and integration with existing systems.

Each of these stages poses its unique challenges and requires specialized knowledge and skills. This section aims to equip ML practitioners with the insights and tools necessary to navigate these complexities, ensuring a smooth and efficient journey from data collection to model deployment. Through a blend of theoretical knowledge and practical insights, this section serves as a roadmap for successfully transforming data into actionable and reliable ML solutions.

8.1 Techniques in Feature Engineering

Feature engineering is a critical yet often underappreciated aspect of machine learning, playing a pivotal role in the success of ML models. This section focuses on the art and science of transforming raw data into informative features that enhance the performance of ML models. This section delves into the methodologies for identifying and creating effective features, explores various techniques for dimensionality reduction and feature selection, and discusses approaches for handling different types of data such as categorical and continuous. Mastering feature engineering is essential for ML practitioners as it directly influences the model's ability to learn patterns and make accurate predictions.

8.1.1 Identifying and Creating Effective Features

The process of identifying and creating effective features involves several key steps:

Domain Knowledge: Leverage domain expertise to identify potential features that could be predictive of the outcome. Understanding the problem domain is crucial in crafting meaningful features.

Data Exploration: Perform exploratory data analysis (EDA) to understand the data distribution, detect anomalies, and uncover relationships between variables.

Feature Creation: Create new features through techniques like feature interaction, where combining two or more features can provide additional insight, or by deriving new features from existing ones (e.g., extracting day of the week from a date).

8.1.2 Dimensionality Reduction and Feature Selection Methods

With high-dimensional data, dimensionality reduction and feature selection become vital:

Dimensionality Reduction: Techniques like Principal Component Analysis (PCA) and t-Distributed Stochastic Neighbor Embedding (t-SNE) reduce the number of features while retaining most of the information. This simplifies the model and can improve performance.

Feature Selection: Use methods like mutual information, chi-square tests, and recursive feature elimination to select a subset of relevant features, removing redundant or irrelevant ones.

8.1.3 Handling Categorical and Continuous Data

Different techniques are required for handling categorical and continuous data:

Categorical Data: Techniques include one-hot encoding, where categorical values are converted into binary vectors, and label encoding, where each category is assigned a unique integer.

Continuous Data: Continuous data may need normalization or standardization to bring all features to the same scale, improving model training efficiency.

Handling Missing Values: For both categorical and continuous data, strategies for handling missing values are crucial. Options include imputation, where missing values are replaced with statistical measures (mean, median, mode), or using algorithms that can handle missing values inherently.

Feature engineering is a vital process that significantly influences the performance of ML models. By effectively identifying and creating features, applying dimensionality reduction and feature selection methods, and adeptly handling different types of data, practitioners can build more accurate, efficient, and robust ML models. This section provides the foundational knowledge and practical strategies necessary to excel in this crucial aspect of machine learning.

8.2 Strategies for Model Development

Model development is a crucial phase in the machine learning pipeline, where theoretical data science meets practical application. This section provides a comprehensive look at the methodologies and best practices for building robust ML models. This section covers the fundamental approaches to constructing effective models, strategies for balancing model complexity with generalizability, and the critical processes of cross-validation and hyperparameter tuning. These strategies are key to developing models that not only perform well on training data but also generalize effectively to new, unseen data, ensuring their usefulness in real-world applications.

8.2.1 Approaches for Building Robust ML Models

Developing robust ML models involves several important approaches:

Understanding the Problem: Clearly define the problem and understand the data. This includes recognizing the type of problem (classification, regression, etc.) and the nature of the data.

Selecting the Right Algorithm: Choose an appropriate ML algorithm based on the problem type, data characteristics, and the desired outcome.

Data Preprocessing: Ensure the data is cleaned, normalized, and transformed properly to maximize the efficiency and effectiveness of the model.

Feature Engineering: Enhance the model's performance by selecting and engineering the right features from the data.

8.2.2 Balancing Model Complexity and Generalizability

Finding the right balance between model complexity and generalizability is crucial:

Avoiding Overfitting: Overly complex models may perform exceptionally well on training data but poorly on new data. Techniques like regularization can help prevent overfitting.

Simplicity and Interpretability: Sometimes, simpler models are more desirable, especially when interpretability is important. Simple models can also be more efficient and less resource-intensive.

Ensuring Generalizability: Use validation techniques to ensure the model generalizes well to new data. This involves testing the model on a separate dataset not used during training.

8.2.3 Cross-Validation and Hyperparameter Tuning

Cross-validation and hyperparameter tuning are essential in fine-tuning the model:

Cross-Validation: Use cross-validation methods, such as k-fold cross-validation, to assess how the model performs on unseen data. This helps in estimating the model's effectiveness and generalizability.

Hyperparameter Tuning: Experiment with different hyperparameter settings to find the optimal combination for the model. Techniques like grid search or random search can be used for systematic hyperparameter optimization.

Automated Hyperparameter Tuning: Consider using automated tools like Bayesian optimization for more efficient hyperparameter tuning.

The strategies for model development are key to building effective and reliable ML models. By carefully approaching model building, balancing complexity with generalizability, and rigorously fine-tuning the model through cross-validation and hyperparameter optimization, practitioners can develop models that are not only accurate but also robust and applicable to a wide range of real-world scenarios. This section provides a foundational framework and practical guidance for achieving success in the complex yet rewarding process of ML model development.

8.3 Best Practices in Model Deployment

Model deployment is the phase where machine learning (ML) theory is put into practical, real-world action. This section explores the crucial aspects of deploying ML models effectively and sustainably. This section discusses strategies to ensure model reliability and scalability, the importance of continuous integration and deployment, and the necessity of ongoing monitoring and maintenance. Deployment is a critical step in the ML lifecycle, where models are transitioned from a controlled development environment to dynamic, real-world applications. Understanding these best practices is essential for practitioners to ensure that their ML solutions deliver consistent, accurate, and efficient performance post-deployment.

8.3.1 Ensuring Model Reliability and Scalability in Production

Key considerations for reliable and scalable model deployment include:

Testing for Reliability: Rigorously test the model in an environment that closely simulates the production setting to ensure its reliability. This includes stress testing the model under various conditions and scenarios.

Scalable Infrastructure: Ensure that the infrastructure supporting the model can handle scale, particularly in terms of handling increased data loads and concurrent requests. This might involve using cloud services or scalable server architectures.

Version Control: Maintain version control for models to manage different iterations effectively and rollback if necessary.

8.3.2 Continuous Integration and Deployment for ML Models

Adopting a continuous integration and deployment (CI/CD) approach can significantly enhance the deployment process:

Automated Testing and Deployment: Implement CI/CD pipelines that automatically test and deploy models. This ensures that any updates or changes to the model are systematically evaluated and integrated.

Iterative Improvement: CI/CD allows for the iterative improvement of models, where updates can be continuously integrated without disrupting the service.

Consistency and Efficiency: This approach ensures consistency in deployment processes and improves the efficiency of rolling out updates or new models.

8.3.3 Monitoring and Maintenance of Deployed Models

Post-deployment, monitoring and maintenance are critical to ensure the ongoing effectiveness of ML models:

Performance Monitoring: Continuously monitor the model's performance to ensure it maintains accuracy and efficiency. Key metrics might include prediction accuracy, response times, and error rates.

Updating and Retraining: Regularly update and retrain models with new data to ensure they remain relevant and accurate, especially in rapidly changing environments.

Anomaly Detection: Implement anomaly detection mechanisms to quickly identify and address any unexpected model behavior or degradation in performance.

Feedback Loops: Establish feedback loops to collect insights from the model's performance and user interactions, which can be used for further refinement and improvement.

Model deployment is a complex and ongoing process that extends beyond simply placing a model into production. It encompasses ensuring the model's reliability and scalability, integrating continuous deployment practices, and setting up robust monitoring and maintenance systems. By adhering to these best practices, ML practitioners can ensure their models not only function as intended in the real world but also adapt and evolve over time, continuing to deliver value and insights.

Chapter 9: Managing Infrastructure and Tooling for MLOps

In the intricate and fast-paced realm of machine learning, the emergence of Machine Learning Operations (MLOps) represents a significant evolution in how ML projects are executed and managed. This chapter delves deep into the crucial aspects of establishing and maintaining the infrastructure and tools necessary for effective MLOps. This exploration is not just about the technical setup; it's about understanding how the right infrastructure and tooling can streamline ML workflows, enhance collaboration, and ensure the efficient deployment and scaling of ML models.

MLOps, a compound of ML and operations, borrows from the philosophy of DevOps, integrating ML system development (Dev) and ML system operation (Ops). It aims to automate and streamline the ML lifecycle, from data preparation and model training to deployment and monitoring, in a consistent, reproducible, and scalable manner. This approach is crucial for organizations looking to deploy ML models at scale and with high efficiency.

In this section, we begin by examining the core components of infrastructure required for MLOps. This includes considerations for computational resources, such as CPUs, GPUs, and TPUs, and how to balance on-premise versus cloud-based solutions. We also explore data storage solutions, network architecture, and the importance of scalable and flexible infrastructure to accommodate the dynamic nature of ML projects.

Next, we delve into the tooling aspect, crucial for the successful implementation of MLOps. This covers a wide range of tools for version control, continuous integration and deployment (CI/CD), automated testing, and monitoring. The choice of tools is pivotal in creating an ecosystem that supports the rapid development, deployment, and iteration of ML models.

Furthermore, we address the challenges associated with managing MLOps infrastructure and tooling, such as ensuring security and compliance, managing costs, and selecting the right tools that align with the organization's needs and goals. Strategies for overcoming these challenges, such as adopting a hybrid cloud approach or utilizing containerization and orchestration tools like Docker and Kubernetes, are also explored.

This chapter provides an extensive guide to setting up and managing the backbone of MLOps. It highlights how the right infrastructure and tooling are instrumental in optimizing ML workflows, enhancing team collaboration, and ensuring the successful deployment and scaling of ML solutions. For organizations and practitioners in the field of ML, this section offers invaluable insights into building and maintaining a robust, efficient, and flexible MLOps environment.

9.1 Infrastructure with Kubernetes for Container Orchestration

The modern landscape of machine learning operations demands robust and scalable infrastructure solutions, and Kubernetes has emerged as a key player in this arena. This section dives into how Kubernetes, a powerful open-source platform, is revolutionizing the orchestration of containerized ML applications. This section provides a thorough exploration of setting up Kubernetes environments, optimizing these setups for ML workloads, and adhering to best practices in Kubernetes management. Kubernetes not only simplifies deployment and scaling but also brings in efficiency and consistency, making it an indispensable tool in the management of complex ML workflows.

9.1.1 Setting Up Kubernetes Environments
Setting up a Kubernetes environment involves several key steps:

Choosing the Right Platform: Decide between self-hosted Kubernetes, managed services like Google Kubernetes Engine (GKE), Amazon Elastic Kubernetes Service (EKS), or Azure Kubernetes Service (AKS) based on your requirements and resources.

Cluster Configuration: Configure the Kubernetes cluster, which includes setting up master and worker nodes, ensuring proper network settings, and configuring storage options.

Security Settings: Implement robust security measures, including setting up role-based access control (RBAC), securing API access, and managing secrets effectively.

Monitoring and Logging: Set up monitoring and logging tools to keep track of the cluster's health and performance, and to troubleshoot issues.

9.1.2 Optimizing Kubernetes for ML Workloads
Kubernetes can be optimized for ML workloads in several ways:

Resource Allocation: Efficiently allocate resources like CPU, GPU, and memory to ML workloads, ensuring that models have enough power for training and inference.

Scalability: Utilize Kubernetes' scalability features to automatically scale ML workloads based on demand, which is particularly crucial for handling varying loads in ML applications.

Pipeline Orchestration: Integrate tools like Kubeflow, which streamline the deployment of ML pipelines on Kubernetes, simplifying the process of running ML models at scale.

9.1.3 Best Practices in Kubernetes Management
Effective management of Kubernetes for ML involves adhering to best practices:

Regular Updates: Keep the Kubernetes environment updated with the latest versions and patches to ensure security and efficiency.

Efficient Load Balancing: Implement load balancing to distribute ML workloads evenly across the cluster, optimizing the utilization of resources.

Disaster Recovery: Plan for disaster recovery with regular backups of the Kubernetes cluster state and critical data, ensuring quick recovery in case of failures.

Documentation and Training: Maintain comprehensive documentation of the Kubernetes setup and provide training to team members, ensuring smooth operations and knowledge sharing.

Kubernetes offers a powerful solution for orchestrating containerized ML workloads, bringing in unparalleled scalability, efficiency, and consistency. By effectively setting up, optimizing, and managing

Kubernetes environments, ML practitioners and organizations can greatly enhance their ML operational capabilities, ensuring seamless deployment and management of complex ML applications.

9.2 Scaling and Securing ML Applications

In the rapidly evolving domain of machine learning, the scalability and security of ML applications are paramount to their success and sustainability. This section addresses the critical strategies for effectively scaling ML systems, ensuring their security, and optimizing their performance. This section delves into the methodologies to handle increasing workloads and user demands, the best practices for safeguarding ML applications against potential threats, and the techniques for performance tuning and monitoring. As ML applications become more integrated into various aspects of business and technology, their ability to scale securely and perform efficiently under varying conditions is crucial.

9.2.1 Strategies for Scaling ML Systems

Effective scaling of ML systems involves several key strategies:

Horizontal vs. Vertical Scaling: Determine whether to scale horizontally (adding more machines) or vertically (adding more power to existing machines) based on the application's needs and resource availability.

Load Balancing: Implement load balancing to distribute the workload evenly across multiple servers, ensuring no single server becomes a bottleneck.

Elasticity: Use cloud-based solutions that offer elasticity, automatically scaling resources up or down as needed based on the workload.

Distributed Computing: Leverage distributed computing frameworks like Apache Spark for data processing, which are essential for handling large-scale ML workloads.

9.2.2 Securing Machine Learning Applications

Securing ML applications is a multi-faceted task that requires comprehensive approaches:

Data Security: Protect sensitive data used by ML models both in transit and at rest. Implement encryption, access controls, and secure data storage practices.

Model Security: Safeguard ML models from adversarial attacks, model theft, and reverse engineering. Techniques like model hardening and differential privacy can be effective.

Compliance and Privacy: Adhere to regulatory and privacy standards, such as GDPR for data privacy, ensuring the ML applications comply with legal and ethical guidelines.

9.2.3 Performance Tuning and Monitoring

Optimizing and monitoring the performance of ML systems is vital for their efficiency and reliability:

Performance Tuning: Regularly tune the performance of ML applications by optimizing algorithms, refining data processing methods, and selecting the right hardware resources.

Monitoring Tools: Utilize monitoring tools to track the application's performance metrics, like throughput, latency, and error rates. Tools like Prometheus, Grafana, or cloud-based solutions can provide comprehensive monitoring capabilities.

Anomaly Detection: Implement anomaly detection mechanisms to identify and address performance issues proactively.

Scaling and securing ML applications are critical aspects that require strategic planning, rigorous implementation, and continuous monitoring. By embracing scalable architectures, ensuring robust security measures, and maintaining optimized performance, ML practitioners and organizations can ensure that their ML systems are not only effective and efficient but also resilient and reliable in the face of growing demands and evolving challenges.

9.3 Advanced Techniques in MLOps

The field of Machine Learning Operations (MLOps) is rapidly evolving, incorporating advanced techniques to streamline and enhance the efficiency of machine learning processes. This section delves into the sophisticated methodologies and optimizations that drive the development of robust, efficient, and scalable ML systems. This section explores cutting-edge ML techniques, engineering strategies for building high-performance ML systems, and advanced topics in model optimization and deployment. These advanced techniques are pivotal in addressing the complex challenges faced in modern ML projects, ensuring that ML systems are not only functional but also optimized for peak performance and scalability.

9.3.1 Advanced ML Techniques and Optimizations

Incorporating advanced ML techniques and optimizations involves:

Automated Machine Learning (AutoML): AutoML tools automate the process of selecting, optimizing, and training ML models, significantly reducing the time and expertise required.

Hyperparameter Optimization: Advanced hyperparameter tuning techniques, such as Bayesian optimization, provide a systematic approach to finding the most effective model parameters.

Parallel and Distributed Training: Leveraging parallel processing and distributed training techniques to handle large datasets and complex models more efficiently.

9.3.2 Engineering Robust, Efficient, and Scalable ML Systems

Engineering ML systems that are robust, efficient, and scalable requires:

Scalable Architecture: Designing ML systems with scalable architecture, such as microservices, to handle increased loads and facilitate maintenance and updates.

Efficiency in Data Processing: Implementing efficient data processing pipelines to handle large volumes of data with minimal latency.

Resource Management: Effective management of computational resources, including the use of GPUs and TPUs for intensive ML tasks.

9.3.3 Advanced Topics: Model Optimization and Deployment Strategies

Advanced model optimization and deployment strategies encompass:

Model Compression and Pruning: Techniques like model compression and pruning to reduce model size and complexity without significantly sacrificing performance, essential for deploying models in resource-constrained environments.

Continuous Deployment and A/B Testing: Implementing continuous deployment pipelines and A/B testing strategies to iteratively improve ML models in production.

Edge Computing in ML: Utilizing edge computing for deploying ML models closer to the data source, reducing latency, and improving response times in real-time applications.

Advanced techniques in MLOps are essential for navigating the complexities and challenges of modern ML projects. By adopting advanced ML techniques, engineering efficient and scalable systems, and employing sophisticated model optimization and deployment strategies, ML practitioners and organizations can build ML systems that are not only technically sound but also strategically optimized for future growth and scalability. These advanced techniques represent the cutting edge of MLOps, driving innovation and efficiency in the field of machine learning.

Chapter 10: Opensource Platforms for Machine Learning

In the rapidly evolving world of machine learning, open-source platforms have become integral to the advancement and democratization of ML technologies. This chapter offers an in-depth exploration of these platforms, highlighting how they have become instrumental in fostering innovation, collaboration, and accessibility in the field of ML. This section delves into the myriad of open-source ML platforms available today, each offering unique tools, libraries, and communities that support the development and deployment of ML models.

These platforms range from comprehensive frameworks designed for building and training sophisticated ML models to more specialized tools focused on particular aspects of ML, such as data visualization, model tuning, or algorithm optimization. Open-source platforms have the distinct advantage of being developed and maintained by communities of experts and enthusiasts, ensuring a wealth of resources, continuous updates, and a support structure that is invaluable for both novice and experienced ML practitioners.

The exploration of these platforms is not just a survey of their capabilities but also an insight into how they contribute to the ML lifecycle. This includes their role in facilitating robust model development, enabling efficient data processing and analysis, and providing scalable solutions for deploying ML models. Additionally, the section examines how these platforms are shaping the future of ML, with their ability to integrate with emerging technologies and adapt to the changing dynamics of the field.

This chapter is a comprehensive guide to the open-source tools that are shaping the landscape of ML. It is an essential resource for anyone looking to navigate the vast and dynamic world of ML, providing the knowledge and insights needed to leverage these platforms effectively. Whether for academic research, industry applications, or personal projects, this section underscores the significance of open-source platforms in driving the growth and accessibility of ML technologies.

10.1 Overview of Open-Source ML Platforms

The landscape of machine learning is richly diverse and constantly evolving, with open-source platforms playing a pivotal role in this transformation. This section provides a comprehensive survey of the various open-source platforms available in the ML domain, shedding light on their features, capabilities, and how they compare against each other. This section aims to offer a clear perspective on the wide array of tools at the disposal of ML practitioners, highlighting how these platforms can be leveraged to develop, train, and deploy ML models effectively.

10.1.1 Surveying the Landscape of Open-Source ML Platforms

The open-source ML landscape encompasses a variety of platforms, each designed to meet specific needs:

General-Purpose ML Libraries: Libraries like TensorFlow, PyTorch, and Scikit-learn offer a broad range of functionalities for different ML tasks, from deep learning to more traditional ML algorithms.

Specialized Platforms: Platforms such as NLTK for natural language processing and OpenCV for computer vision focus on specific ML domains, providing specialized tools and functionalities.

Data Processing and Visualization Tools: Tools like Pandas, NumPy, and Matplotlib play a crucial role in data preprocessing and visualization, which are essential steps in the ML pipeline.

10.1.2 Features and Capabilities of Key ML Platforms

Key open-source ML platforms are characterized by their unique features and capabilities:

TensorFlow: Known for its flexibility and extensive functionality, TensorFlow is ideal for deep learning applications and provides robust support for distributed computing.

PyTorch: PyTorch is appreciated for its dynamic computation graph and user-friendly interface, making it popular in the research community for prototyping and experimentation.

Scikit-learn: With its simple and accessible interface, Scikit-learn is perfect for implementing traditional ML algorithms and is widely used in educational and small to medium-scale projects.

10.1.3 Comparative Overview of Popular ML Platforms

Comparing these platforms involves looking at various factors:

Ease of Use: Platforms like Keras and Scikit-learn are known for their ease of use, making them suitable for beginners and rapid prototyping.

Performance and Scalability: TensorFlow and PyTorch are highly scalable and performant, making them suitable for complex and large-scale ML applications.

Community and Ecosystem: The size and activity of a platform's community can significantly impact the support, resources, and continuous development of the platform.

Specialization: Some platforms are tailored for specific tasks, offering specialized tools that are more efficient for those particular applications.

The open-source ML platform landscape offers a rich array of tools for practitioners, catering to a wide range of needs and preferences. By understanding the features, capabilities, and differences of these platforms, ML developers and researchers can make informed choices about the tools that will best suit their specific project requirements. This comparative overview serves as a guide for navigating the diverse and dynamic field of ML, enabling practitioners to harness the power of these platforms effectively.

10.2 Setup and Customization of Open-Source ML Platforms

Setting up and customizing open-source machine learning platforms is a crucial step in the ML workflow, one that can significantly influence the efficiency and effectiveness of ML projects. This section focuses on providing practical guidance for installing these platforms, tailoring them to meet specific project requirements, and integrating them seamlessly with existing systems. This section is designed to assist ML practitioners in navigating the initial setup process, customizing the platforms to fit their unique use cases, and ensuring compatibility with their current technological infrastructure.

10.2.1 Step by Step Guide for Platform Setup

A typical setup process for open-source ML platforms involves several key steps:

System Requirements: First, ensure that your system meets the necessary requirements for the chosen platform, including hardware specifications and operating system compatibility.

Installation: Follow the official documentation for the installation process. This often involves downloading the platform package and using package managers like pip for Python libraries (e.g., `pip install tensorflow`).

Environment Setup: Setting up a virtual environment using tools like venv or conda is recommended to manage dependencies and isolate your ML project environment.

Verification: After installation, run a simple test script to verify that the platform is installed correctly and is functioning as expected.

10.2.2 Customizing ML Platforms for Specific Needs
Customizing an ML platform involves:

Configuration for Performance: Optimize the configuration of the platform to utilize the available hardware resources effectively, such as configuring TensorFlow to use GPU acceleration.

Custom Libraries and Extensions: Depending on the project needs, you might need to install additional libraries or extensions that complement the core platform.

User-Defined Functions and Modules: Create custom functions and modules to handle specific tasks unique to your project, enhancing the platform's capabilities.

10.2.3 Integrating Open-Source Platforms with Existing Systems
Effective integration of ML platforms with existing systems is critical:

Data Integration: Ensure that the platform can effectively interact with your existing data sources and formats. This might involve writing custom data loaders or using APIs for data extraction.

Compatibility with Existing Software Stack: Check for compatibility issues with the existing software stack, and make necessary adjustments to ensure smooth integration.

Automated Workflow Integration: Integrate the platform into your automated workflows, such as CI/CD pipelines, for efficient development and deployment processes.

The setup and customization of open-source ML platforms are foundational steps in preparing for successful ML projects. By following a structured approach to installation, tailoring the platforms to specific project needs, and ensuring seamless integration with existing systems, ML practitioners can create a robust and efficient environment for developing and deploying ML models. This section provides the guidance needed to navigate these processes, ensuring a solid foundation for leveraging the power of open-source ML platforms.

10.3 Community Support and Ecosystem
The success and dynamism of open-source machine learning platforms are significantly bolstered by their vibrant communities and ecosystems. This section explores the crucial role these communities play in the development and advancement of open-source ML technologies. This section delves into navigating the open-source ML community, ways to collaborate and contribute to these projects, and

how to leverage the vast pool of community knowledge and resources. The strength of open-source platforms lies not just in their technical capabilities but also in the collaborative and supportive environment fostered by their users and contributors.

10.3.1 Navigating the Open-Source Community for ML

Engaging with the open-source community involves several strategies:

Joining Forums and Mailing Lists: Participate in forums, mailing lists, and online communities where developers and users discuss the platform, share insights, and resolve issues.

Attending Workshops and Conferences: Attend workshops, webinars, and conferences dedicated to open-source ML platforms. These events are great for learning, networking, and staying updated with the latest developments.

Online Tutorials and Documentation: Utilize the extensive range of tutorials, documentation, and educational resources available online to deepen your understanding of the platforms.

10.3.2 Collaborating and Contributing to ML Open-Source Projects

Contributing to open-source projects is a valuable way to engage with the community:

Contributing Code: You can contribute to the project by fixing bugs, adding new features, or improving existing functionalities. This usually involves submitting pull requests on platforms like GitHub.

Documentation and Tutorials: Contribute by writing or improving documentation, creating tutorials, or developing educational content to help new users.

Issue Reporting and Testing: Participate in the community by reporting issues, participating in testing new releases, and providing feedback to the developers.

10.3.3 Leveraging Community Knowledge and Resources

The open-source community is a rich resource for knowledge and support:

Seeking Help and Advice: Leverage community forums and Q&A sites to seek help, ask questions, and get advice from experienced users and developers.

Sharing Experiences and Best Practices: Share your own experiences, insights, and best practices with the community, contributing to the collective knowledge.

Staying Informed: Stay informed about the latest updates, trends, and best practices by following key community figures, blogs, and social media channels related to the ML platform.

The community support and ecosystem surrounding open-source ML platforms are invaluable assets. By actively navigating and participating in these communities, individuals and organizations can not only enhance their own ML endeavors but also contribute to the collective growth and improvement of open-source ML technologies. Engaging with these communities allows for a richer, more collaborative, and more innovative experience in the world of machine learning.

Chapter 11: Using AWS for ML Solutions

In the realm of machine learning, cloud platforms like Amazon Web Services have emerged as powerful enablers, offering a vast array of services and tools that cater to various aspects of ML project development. This chapter provides a comprehensive exploration of how AWS can be leveraged to design, implement, and scale ML solutions effectively. This section is dedicated to unraveling the suite of ML-focused services and features offered by AWS, illustrating how they can be integrated into ML workflows to enhance efficiency, scalability, and performance.

From data storage and processing to model training and deployment, AWS offers an end-to-end ecosystem that simplifies and accelerates the ML lifecycle. This exploration is not just about the technical capabilities of AWS but also about understanding how these services fit into the broader context of ML projects. It addresses the ways in which AWS simplifies complex tasks, such as handling large datasets, managing compute resources, and deploying ML models at scale.

For practitioners and organizations venturing into ML, AWS presents an opportunity to leverage cloud computing's power and flexibility. This section will guide readers through the various AWS services pertinent to ML, such as Amazon Sagemaker for model building and training, AWS Lambda for serverless computing, and Amazon EC2 for scalable computing capacity. It will also cover key considerations for using AWS in ML projects, including cost management, security features, and best practices for cloud-based ML deployments.

This chapter aims to provide a thorough understanding of how AWS's cloud infrastructure and services can be harnessed to drive ML projects. This exploration is crucial for anyone looking to leverage cloud computing for ML, offering insights into how AWS can serve as a powerful and efficient platform for building and deploying ML solutions.

11.1 Utilizing AWS AI Services for Building ML Solutions

Amazon Web Services offers a comprehensive suite of AI services that are revolutionizing the way machine learning solutions are built and deployed. "Utilizing AWS AI Services for Building ML Solutions" dives into the array of AI and ML services provided by AWS, providing a roadmap for leveraging these tools in various ML projects. This section offers an overview of AWS's AI services, a step-by-step guide to their implementation, and insights on optimizing these services for different ML scenarios. For ML practitioners and organizations, understanding and effectively utilizing AWS's AI services can significantly enhance the efficiency, scalability, and sophistication of their ML solutions.

11.1.1 Overview of AWS AI Services for Machine Learning

AWS provides a range of AI services tailored for ML applications:

Amazon SageMaker: A comprehensive service that enables data scientists and developers to build, train, and deploy ML models at scale. SageMaker offers a fully managed environment with tools for every step of the ML lifecycle.

AWS Rekognition: A service for image and video analysis, utilizing deep learning to identify objects, people, text, and activities.

Amazon Comprehend: A natural language processing (NLP) service that uses machine learning to uncover insights and relationships in text.

Amazon Lex: A service for building conversational interfaces into applications using voice and text, powered by the same technology as Alexa.

Amazon Polly: A text-to-speech service that turns text into lifelike speech.

11.1.2 Step by Step Guide to Implementing AWS ML Tools

Implementing AWS ML tools involves several key steps:

Initial Setup: Start by setting up an AWS account and accessing the AWS Management Console. Ensure you have the necessary permissions to use the ML services.

Selecting the Right Service: Based on your ML project requirements, select the appropriate AWS AI service. For instance, choose SageMaker for custom model building and training or use pre-built models from Rekognition or Comprehend for specific tasks.

Data Preparation: Prepare your data according to the service requirements. AWS provides tools for data storage (Amazon S3) and processing (AWS Glue).

Model Development and Training: For custom models, use SageMaker to develop and train your model. SageMaker provides Jupyter notebooks, built-in algorithms, and support for popular ML frameworks.

Deployment and Testing: Deploy your model using AWS services. Test the deployed model to ensure it meets your application's requirements.

11.1.3 Optimizing AWS AI Services for Different ML Scenarios

Optimizing AWS AI services requires a tailored approach depending on the scenario:

Performance Tuning: For compute-intensive tasks, optimize your resource allocation in SageMaker, selecting the right instance types and managing resource utilization effectively.

Cost Optimization: Keep an eye on the costs associated with AWS services. Use AWS cost management tools to track and optimize expenses.

Scalability: Leverage AWS's scalability features to handle varying workloads, especially for services that experience fluctuating levels of demand.

Security and Compliance: Utilize AWS's security features, such as encryption and access control, to protect your data and models, ensuring compliance with regulatory standards.

AWS's AI services provide a robust and flexible platform for building and deploying a wide range of ML solutions. By following a structured approach to implementation and optimization, ML practitioners can harness the full potential of these services, creating sophisticated, scalable, and efficient ML solutions that cater to a diverse array of use cases.

11.2 Best Practices for Leveraging AWS for ML

Amazon Web Services offers an expansive ecosystem for machine learning projects, but navigating this landscape effectively requires a strategic approach. This section aims to provide insights into how to use

AWS resources efficiently, ensure security and compliance, and scale ML solutions effectively. This section is designed to help ML practitioners and organizations optimize their AWS usage for ML projects, aligning with best practices to maximize the benefits while managing costs and maintaining robust security.

11.2.1 Efficient Use of AWS Resources in ML Projects

Maximizing efficiency in the use of AWS resources involves several key practices:

Right-Sizing Resources: Carefully assess and select the appropriate types and sizes of AWS instances based on the computational needs of your ML projects. Utilize AWS's instance types that are optimized for ML, like those equipped with GPUs for deep learning tasks.

Cost Management: Keep track of expenses using AWS Cost Management tools. Implement cost-saving measures such as using Spot Instances for non-critical, interruptible tasks, and shutting down instances when not in use.

Utilizing AWS Managed Services: Leverage AWS managed services like Amazon SageMaker, which simplifies the ML workflow, from model building and training to deployment and monitoring.

11.2.2 Security and Compliance in AWS ML Environments

Security and compliance are paramount, especially when dealing with sensitive data:

Data Protection: Implement encryption for data at rest and in transit. Use services like AWS Key Management Service (KMS) for managing encryption keys.

Access Control: Utilize AWS Identity and Access Management (IAM) to control access to AWS services and resources securely. Implement least privilege access principles.

Compliance: Ensure that your ML solutions comply with industry standards and regulations. AWS offers compliance resources like the AWS Compliance Center to help you understand relevant requirements.

11.2.3 Scaling ML Solutions on AWS

Scaling ML solutions efficiently on AWS requires a strategic approach:

Auto Scaling: Use AWS Auto Scaling to adjust resources automatically in response to changing demand. This is crucial for ML applications with variable workloads.

Elasticity: Take advantage of the elastic nature of AWS cloud infrastructure. Scale up resources during high-demand periods and scale down during low-usage times to optimize costs.

Distributed Training: For large-scale ML training tasks, use distributed training approaches that leverage multiple instances to reduce training time.

Leveraging AWS for ML involves more than just using its services; it requires a strategic approach to resource management, security, and scalability. By following these best practices, ML practitioners and organizations can ensure that they are using AWS resources efficiently, maintaining robust security and compliance, and scaling their ML solutions effectively. This approach allows them to harness the full potential of AWS in their ML endeavors, driving innovation and achieving their project goals more effectively.

11.3 Case Studies and Practical Examples

Amazon Web Services has been instrumental in powering a wide array of successful machine learning projects across various industries. This section offers an insightful exploration into real-world applications of AWS for ML, showcasing success stories, valuable lessons learned, and tangible results achieved. This section serves as a practical guide, providing inspiring examples and insights that illustrate the effectiveness of AWS in deploying ML solutions. These case studies are invaluable for understanding how AWS tools and services can be applied to solve complex problems, scale ML applications, and drive innovation.

11.3.1 Success Stories of ML Implementations on AWS

Numerous organizations have leveraged AWS to drive successful ML implementations:

Healthcare Diagnostics: AWS has been used to develop advanced diagnostic tools that leverage ML for quicker and more accurate disease detection, significantly impacting patient care and treatment outcomes.

Financial Fraud Detection: Financial institutions have implemented ML models on AWS to detect and prevent fraudulent activities, enhancing security and customer trust.

Retail Personalization: E-commerce platforms have utilized AWS to create personalized shopping experiences for customers using ML, leading to increased customer satisfaction and sales.

11.3.2 Lessons Learned from AWS ML Deployments

Key lessons from deploying ML solutions on AWS include:

Scalability Planning: One of the most critical lessons is the importance of planning for scalability from the outset. Successful deployments have shown the need to design ML systems that can grow and adapt as data volumes and computational needs increase.

Data Security and Privacy: Ensuring the security and privacy of data used in ML models is paramount. Deployments have highlighted the importance of using AWS security and encryption tools to protect sensitive information.

Cost Optimization: Efficient use of AWS resources is essential for managing costs. Lessons from various projects emphasize the importance of monitoring and optimizing AWS usage to prevent unnecessary expenses.

11.3.3 Real-world Applications and Results

Real-world applications of AWS in ML have yielded significant results:

Predictive Maintenance in Manufacturing: ML models hosted on AWS have been used for predictive maintenance in manufacturing, reducing downtime and maintenance costs.

Content Recommendation Engines: Media companies have built sophisticated recommendation engines on AWS, improving user engagement and content consumption.

Natural Language Processing for Customer Service: Businesses have implemented NLP solutions on AWS to enhance customer service interactions, using chatbots and automated response systems.

The case studies and practical examples of ML implementations on AWS provide a wealth of knowledge and inspiration. They demonstrate the platform's capabilities in handling diverse and complex ML tasks, offering insights into effective strategies and common pitfalls. These real-world examples not only showcase the power of AWS in driving ML initiatives but also serve as a guide for practitioners and organizations looking to embark on their own ML journeys using AWS.

Chapter 12: Data Science Framework for ML Services

In the intricate and multidisciplinary world of machine learning (ML), the establishment of a robust data science framework is essential for the successful deployment and maintenance of ML services. "Data Science Framework for ML Services" delves into the comprehensive structure and methodologies that constitute the backbone of effective ML service implementation. This exploration is centered around the integration of various data science elements — from data collection and preprocessing to model development, validation, and deployment — within a cohesive framework that optimally supports ML services.

The data science framework for ML services is not just a set of isolated technical tasks; it represents a holistic approach that encompasses data management, algorithm selection, computational considerations, and post-deployment monitoring and updates. It's about creating a sustainable ecosystem where data science components work in synergy to produce reliable, efficient, and impactful ML services.

In this section, we begin by exploring the foundational aspects of the data science framework, which include identifying key data sources, ensuring data quality, and preparing data in a manner that's conducive to effective ML. This includes the use of advanced techniques in data processing and feature engineering, as well as the adoption of best practices in data governance and ethics.

Next, the focus shifts to the development phase, where the selection of appropriate ML models, algorithm training, and the fine-tuning of parameters take place. This phase critically determines the efficacy and accuracy of the ML services, necessitating a careful balance between model complexity and practical utility.

Furthermore, the section delves into the deployment aspect, emphasizing the need for robust deployment strategies that ensure the scalability, reliability, and security of ML services. This includes the integration of the model into existing IT infrastructure, the management of computational resources, and the implementation of continuous integration and deployment pipelines.

Finally, the section addresses the ongoing maintenance and evolution of ML services post-deployment. This involves setting up systems for regular monitoring of model performance, updating models in response to new data or changing conditions, and iteratively improving the services based on feedback and evolving requirements.

This chapter offers a detailed guide on building and managing a comprehensive framework that is fundamental to the success of ML services. This framework serves as a roadmap for organizations and practitioners in the ML field, outlining the critical steps and considerations necessary for creating effective, sustainable, and impactful ML solutions.

12.1 Setting Up Data Science Environment on AWS

Creating a data science environment on Amazon Web Services is a critical step for leveraging the cloud's power for machine learning (ML) and data science projects. This section provides a comprehensive guide on establishing an effective and efficient workspace on AWS, specifically tailored for data science applications. This section covers the essentials of creating a data science workspace on AWS, configuring various AWS services for data science needs, and integrating essential tools and libraries. For data scientists and ML practitioners, understanding how to effectively utilize AWS's vast resources can significantly enhance their analytical capabilities and streamline their workflows.

12.1.1 Creating an Effective AWS Based Data Science Workspace

Setting up an effective data science workspace in AWS involves:

Selecting the Right AWS Services: Begin by choosing the appropriate AWS services for your data science needs. Services like Amazon S3 for data storage, Amazon EC2 for computing, and AWS Glue for data integration are fundamental.

Workspace Setup: Set up a virtual workspace using Amazon SageMaker, which provides a fully managed service with Jupyter notebooks, making it ideal for data exploration, visualization, and model development.

Access Management: Utilize AWS Identity and Access Management (IAM) to securely control access to AWS services and resources, ensuring that your data and resources are protected.

12.1.2 Configuring AWS Services for Data Science

Configuring AWS services for data science involves:

Storage and Database Configuration: Configure Amazon S3 for data storage and choose the appropriate database service (like Amazon RDS or DynamoDB) based on the nature of your data (structured, semi-structured, or unstructured).

Compute Resources: Set up EC2 instances or use AWS Lambda for serverless computing. Choose instances that match your workload requirements, considering factors like memory, CPU, and GPU needs.

Data Processing: Leverage AWS data processing services like AWS Glue and Amazon EMR for data integration, ETL (Extract, Transform, Load) processes, and big data processing.

12.1.3 Integrating Tools and Libraries in AWS

Integrating tools and libraries in your AWS environment is crucial for advanced data science work:

Library Installation: Install necessary data science libraries and frameworks, such as Pandas, NumPy, SciPy, TensorFlow, and PyTorch, on your EC2 instances or within SageMaker.

Tool Integration: Integrate additional tools for version control (like Git), continuous integration/continuous deployment (CI/CD), and project management, to streamline your workflow.

Leveraging AWS Marketplace: Explore AWS Marketplace for third-party data science tools and applications that can be seamlessly integrated into your AWS environment.

Setting up a data science environment on AWS requires thoughtful selection and configuration of AWS services, as well as the integration of essential tools and libraries. By tailoring the AWS environment to the

specific needs of data science and ML projects, practitioners can create a powerful, scalable, and efficient workspace that enhances their capabilities in data analysis and model development. This approach not only streamlines the data science workflow but also leverages the full potential of AWS in driving insightful and impactful data science outcomes.

12.2 Leveraging AWS ML Services for Data Science Projects

Amazon Web Services has become a powerhouse in providing scalable and efficient machine learning services for data science projects. This section delves into the utilization of AWS's comprehensive suite of ML tools and services to enhance data science practices. This section outlines how AWS ML services can be harnessed for advanced analytics, the methodologies for building and training models on AWS, and the strategies for implementing end-to-end data science workflows. For data scientists and ML practitioners, AWS offers a robust platform that can significantly streamline and amplify their data science capabilities.

12.2.1 Harnessing AWS ML Services for Advanced Analytics

AWS offers a variety of services tailored for advanced analytics:

Amazon SageMaker: Provides an integrated development environment for building, training, and deploying ML models. SageMaker's Jupyter Notebook instances, pre-built algorithms, and model tuning capabilities make it a go-to tool for data scientists.

Amazon Redshift: A fast, scalable data warehouse that enables running complex analytics queries across large datasets, seamlessly integrating with business intelligence tools.

AWS Glue: A fully managed ETL (Extract, Transform, Load) service that simplifies data preparation for analytics, offering data cataloging and transformation capabilities.

12.2.2 Building and Training Models on AWS

AWS facilitates efficient model building and training:

Custom Model Development: Utilize EC2 instances, particularly those with GPU support, for developing custom ML models. AWS provides flexibility to work with various ML frameworks, including TensorFlow and PyTorch.

Managed Training Environment: Amazon SageMaker streamlines the training process by managing the underlying infrastructure, allowing data scientists to focus on model building and experimentation.

Optimized Training Operations: AWS offers tools like Amazon SageMaker Automatic Model Tuning to optimize model hyperparameters, improving model accuracy and efficiency.

12.2.3 Implementing End to End Data Science Workflows on AWS

AWS supports the implementation of comprehensive data science workflows:

Data Ingestion and Storage: Leverage services like AWS S3 for data storage and AWS Kinesis for real-time data ingestion and streaming.

Seamless Integration: Integrate various AWS services to create a cohesive workflow, from data ingestion and preprocessing with AWS Glue, to model training with SageMaker, and deployment using AWS Lambda or Amazon ECS for containerized applications.

Monitoring and Maintenance: Utilize AWS CloudWatch for monitoring the performance of deployed models and maintaining the health of the data science workflow.

AWS ML services offer a versatile and powerful toolkit for data science projects, enabling advanced analytics, streamlined model building and training, and the implementation of end-to-end workflows. By leveraging these services, data science practitioners can achieve more scalable, efficient, and effective outcomes, harnessing the full potential of cloud computing and AI technologies in their projects.

12.3 Managing Resources and Cost Optimization

Effective management of resources and cost optimization are crucial for maximizing the efficiency and sustainability of projects on Amazon Web Services (AWS). "Managing Resources and Cost Optimization" focuses on strategic resource management, cost-effective utilization of AWS services, and the monitoring and optimization of AWS resource usage. This section is essential for individuals and organizations looking to leverage AWS for machine learning (ML) and data science projects without incurring unnecessary expenses. It provides insights into balancing performance and cost, ensuring that AWS's powerful resources are used in the most efficient manner possible.

12.3.1 Resource Management Strategies in AWS

Efficient resource management on AWS involves several key strategies:

Right-Sizing Resources: Assess and select the most appropriate AWS resources (such as EC2 instance types, RDS database instances, or S3 storage classes) to match the specific needs of your workload, avoiding over-provisioning.

Elasticity and Scalability: Leverage AWS's elasticity to scale resources up or down based on demand. Use services like Auto Scaling to automatically adjust capacity to maintain steady, predictable performance at the lowest possible cost.

Utilizing Reserved Instances and Savings Plans: For predictable workloads, consider purchasing Reserved Instances or using AWS Savings Plans to save on long-term costs.

12.3.2 Cost Effective Use of AWS Services

To ensure cost-effective use of AWS services:

Budgets and Cost Alarms: Set up budgets and cost alarms using AWS Budgets to monitor and control AWS spending.

Spot Instances for ML Training: Utilize AWS Spot Instances for ML training tasks that are not time-sensitive, reducing costs significantly compared to On-Demand Instances.

Decommissioning Unused Resources: Regularly review and decommission unused or underutilized resources. Ensure that all non-essential instances, volumes, and snapshots are terminated or deleted.

12.3.3 Monitoring and Optimizing AWS Resource Usage

Continuous monitoring and optimization of resource usage are key to managing costs:

AWS Cost Explorer: Use AWS Cost Explorer to visualize and understand your AWS spending patterns, identifying areas where cost savings can be made.

Performance Monitoring: Utilize tools like Amazon CloudWatch to monitor the performance of AWS resources. This helps in identifying over-utilized or under-utilized resources.

Review and Optimize Regularly: Conduct regular reviews of resource usage and optimize configurations. This might include updating instance types, adjusting Auto Scaling policies, or restructuring the architecture to be more cost-effective.

Managing resources and optimizing costs on AWS is a dynamic and ongoing process. By implementing effective resource management strategies, ensuring cost-effective use of services, and continuously monitoring and optimizing resource usage, ML practitioners and organizations can make the most out of AWS for their data science and ML projects. This strategic approach not only helps in minimizing costs but also ensures that AWS resources are utilized to their fullest potential, contributing to the overall success and sustainability of projects.

Chapter 13: Enterprise-Level ML Architectures

In the realm of machine learning, the shift from experimental projects to full-scale enterprise applications marks a significant transition. This chapter delves into the complex world of designing, implementing, and maintaining ML systems at an enterprise scale. This exploration is crucial for understanding how ML can be effectively integrated into larger business processes and systems. It addresses the unique challenges and requirements of deploying ML solutions that not only meet the high-performance standards expected in enterprise environments but also adhere to rigorous scalability, reliability, and security demands.

The journey through this section begins with an examination of the fundamental architectural principles that underpin successful enterprise-level ML deployments. This includes a focus on robust and scalable infrastructure that can handle the vast amounts of data and intensive computational workloads characteristic of enterprise ML applications. The discussion extends to the design patterns and best practices that facilitate the integration of ML into existing enterprise ecosystems, ensuring seamless interaction with legacy systems and adherence to established IT protocols.

Furthermore, this section delves into the critical aspects of data management at an enterprise level. This encompasses strategies for efficient data ingestion, storage, and processing, as well as considerations for data governance, quality control, and compliance with regulatory standards. The architecture must be designed to efficiently manage the lifecycle of data, from collection and preprocessing to model training and inference.

Additionally, the section explores the deployment strategies for ML models in enterprise environments. This includes the implementation of continuous integration and deployment pipelines, model versioning, and A/B testing frameworks to iteratively improve ML models while minimizing disruptions to business operations. Also, it addresses the challenge of deploying ML models at scale, discussing techniques like containerization, microservices, and serverless architectures.

This chapter offers a comprehensive guide to building and managing ML systems in large-scale, complex enterprise environments. It provides insights into the architectural considerations, strategies, and best practices necessary for the successful integration of ML into enterprise systems. For organizations looking to harness the power of ML, this section serves as an essential roadmap, outlining the steps and considerations required to develop effective, scalable, and secure enterprise-level ML solutions.

13.1 Architectural Patterns for Enterprise-Level ML Solutions

Implementing machine learning at the enterprise level necessitates a strategic approach to architecture, one that accommodates scale, robustness, and adaptability. This section offers an in-depth analysis of designing architectures tailored for large-scale ML deployments. This section addresses the key components of scalable and robust ML architectures for enterprises, examines successful case studies, and explores how these architectural patterns can be adapted to meet diverse business needs. For enterprises venturing into ML, these architectural blueprints are essential for building systems that are not only technically proficient but also align with broader business objectives and dynamics.

13.1.1 Designing Scalable and Robust ML Architectures for Enterprises
Key considerations in designing enterprise-level ML architectures include:

Scalability: The architecture should be designed to efficiently handle increasing volumes of data and growing computational demands. This often involves leveraging cloud-based solutions, containerization, and microservices.

Robustness and Reliability: Ensure high availability and fault tolerance. Implementing redundancy, failover mechanisms, and rigorous testing protocols are essential to maintain consistent performance and minimize downtime.

Data Pipeline Integration: Architectures must integrate seamlessly with data pipelines, ensuring efficient data ingestion, preprocessing, and storage. Tools like Apache Kafka for data streaming and Amazon S3 for storage are commonly used.

13.1.2 Case Studies: Successful Enterprise ML Architectural Designs
Analyzing successful case studies provides valuable insights:

Financial Sector ML Deployments: Financial institutions have implemented ML for fraud detection and risk assessment, using architectures that prioritize data security and real-time processing capabilities.

Retail and E-commerce ML Applications: Retail giants leverage ML for personalized recommendations and inventory management, employing architectures that handle massive datasets and support agile, customer-centric models.

Healthcare ML Solutions: Healthcare organizations use ML for predictive diagnostics and patient care optimization. Their architectures often focus on data privacy, integration with existing healthcare systems, and handling diverse data types.

13.1.3 Adapting Architectural Patterns for Diverse Business Needs
Adapting ML architectures to different business contexts involves:

Customization for Specific Industry Requirements: Different industries have unique requirements; for instance, manufacturing might emphasize predictive maintenance, while e-commerce might focus on customer behavior analysis.

Balancing Innovation with Legacy Systems: Integrating ML with existing IT infrastructure while introducing innovative technologies and methodologies.

Flexibility and Modularity: Designing architectures that are flexible and modular, allowing for easy adaptation and scaling as business needs evolve.

The architectural patterns for enterprise-level ML solutions are foundational to the successful deployment and scalability of ML in large organizations. By focusing on designing scalable, robust architectures, learning from successful case studies, and adapting these patterns to specific business needs, enterprises can effectively harness the power of ML. This approach ensures that ML solutions not only drive technological innovation but also align closely with the strategic objectives and operational realities of the business.

13.2 Integrating AWS ML Services into Enterprise Systems

The integration of Amazon Web Services ML services into enterprise systems represents a strategic move for organizations seeking to leverage cloud-based machine learning capabilities. This section explores the methodologies and best practices for seamlessly incorporating AWS's advanced ML services into existing enterprise infrastructures. This section covers the strategies for smooth integration, bridging on-premises systems with AWS ML solutions, and the best practices that ensure successful implementation within an enterprise context. This integration is crucial for enterprises aiming to harness the power of cloud ML technologies while maintaining the integrity and efficiency of their existing systems.

13.2.1 Seamless Integration Strategies for AWS ML Services

Effective integration of AWS ML services into enterprise systems involves:

API-Based Integration: Utilize AWS ML service APIs to integrate cloud-based ML capabilities with existing enterprise applications. For example, incorporating Amazon SageMaker endpoints into business applications for real-time predictions.

Hybrid Cloud Environments: For enterprises not fully in the cloud, adopting a hybrid approach can facilitate gradual integration. AWS offers services like AWS Outposts to extend AWS infrastructure and services to on-premises facilities.

Data Management and Transfer: Implement efficient data transfer mechanisms between on-premises systems and AWS using services like AWS DataSync or AWS Transfer for SFTP.

13.2.2 Bridging On-Premises Systems with AWS ML Solutions

Bridging on-premises systems with AWS entails:

Data Synchronization: Ensure consistent data synchronization between on-premises databases and AWS data storage services, maintaining data integrity and accuracy.

Network Connectivity: Establish secure and reliable network connectivity between on-premises systems and AWS using AWS Direct Connect or VPN connections.

Edge Computing: Use AWS IoT Greengrass or AWS Snowball Edge for edge computing capabilities, allowing data processing closer to the data source, reducing latency for ML applications.

13.2.3 Best Practices for AWS ML Integration in Enterprises

Best practices for integrating AWS ML services include:

Security and Compliance: Adhere to security best practices and compliance requirements. Utilize AWS security tools and services to protect data and ML models.

Scalability and Performance Optimization: Optimize for scalability and performance by choosing the right AWS service configurations and resource types based on the enterprise's workload demands.

Cost Management: Monitor and manage costs effectively using AWS Cost Management tools. Implement cost-optimization strategies like selecting appropriate pricing models (On-Demand, Reserved Instances, or Spot Instances).

Continuous Monitoring and Maintenance: Implement continuous monitoring using services like Amazon CloudWatch and set up a maintenance plan to keep the integrated system efficient and up-to-date.

Integrating AWS ML services into enterprise systems requires a thoughtful approach that considers seamless integration, effective bridging of on-premises and cloud environments, and adherence to best practices in security, scalability, and cost management. By strategically implementing these practices, enterprises can effectively augment their existing systems with AWS's powerful ML capabilities, leading to enhanced efficiency, innovation, and competitive advantage in their business operations.

13.3 Security, Compliance, and Scalability Considerations

In the realm of enterprise-level machine learning solutions, security, compliance, and scalability are paramount considerations that directly impact the success and viability of ML deployments. This section is a comprehensive exploration of these critical aspects, essential for ensuring that enterprise ML solutions are secure, adhere to regulatory standards, and are capable of scaling in response to evolving business needs. This section delves into the strategies and best practices for fortifying ML architectures against security threats, navigating the complex landscape of compliance and regulation, and designing ML systems that are both scalable and flexible.

13.3.1 Ensuring Security in Enterprise ML Solutions

Security in enterprise ML involves several key components:

Data Security: Implement robust measures to protect data, including encryption both at rest and in transit, secure data storage solutions, and access control mechanisms to regulate who can view or modify data.

Model Security: Protect ML models from tampering and unauthorized access. This includes securing model endpoints, implementing authentication for model access, and safeguarding against adversarial attacks.

Infrastructure Security: Ensure that the underlying infrastructure, whether on-premises or cloud-based, is secured against breaches. Regular security audits, penetration testing, and the use of firewalls and intrusion detection systems are crucial practices.

13.3.2 Compliance and Regulatory Aspects in ML Architectures

Adhering to compliance and regulatory standards is essential:

Data Privacy Regulations: Stay compliant with data privacy laws such as GDPR, HIPAA, or CCPA, which dictate how data can be collected, processed, and stored.

Industry-Specific Regulations: Depending on the industry, there may be additional regulations to consider. For example, financial services may need to comply with regulations like SOX or Basel III.

Documentation and Auditing: Maintain thorough documentation of data handling and processing activities and conduct regular audits to ensure ongoing compliance.

13.3.3 Strategies for Scalable and Flexible ML Systems in Enterprises

Developing scalable and flexible ML systems involves:

Modular Architecture: Design ML systems with a modular approach, allowing components to be independently scaled as needed.

Cloud-Based Scalability: Leverage cloud platforms like AWS or Azure, which offer scalability and elasticity to handle varying workloads without the need for substantial upfront investment in physical infrastructure.

Auto-Scaling and Resource Optimization: Implement auto-scaling capabilities to dynamically adjust resources based on demand and optimize resource usage to balance performance with cost.

Flexible Data Management: Design data management strategies that can scale with the growing size and complexity of data sets. This includes the use of scalable databases and data lakes.

Security, compliance, and scalability are critical elements that must be intricately woven into the fabric of enterprise ML solutions. By prioritizing these considerations, enterprises can ensure that their ML systems are not only technically proficient but also secure, compliant with regulatory requirements, and capable of adapting to changing business landscapes. This approach is vital for enterprises to fully harness the power of ML while maintaining trust, integrity, and operational excellence.

Chapter 14: Human Dimensions of ML Governance, Bias, and Privacy

In the intricate tapestry of machine learning, the human dimensions such as governance, bias, and privacy play a pivotal role in shaping ethical, fair, and responsible AI systems. This chapter delves deep into these often-overlooked yet crucial aspects of ML, underscoring the importance of considering the societal, ethical, and human impact of AI technologies. This chapter is not merely a technical overview of ML principles but a thorough exploration of the human-centric issues that intersect with ML development and deployment. It is an essential discourse for understanding how ML systems can be governed with accountability, designed without bias, and executed with a paramount emphasis on privacy.

The chapter opens by navigating the complex landscape of ML governance, exploring how policies, frameworks, and ethical guidelines are essential for overseeing the responsible development and use of ML technologies. It delves into how governance extends beyond mere compliance with laws and regulations, encompassing broader ethical considerations that ensure ML technologies are used for the greater good.

The discussion then shifts to the critical issue of bias in ML, a facet that has profound implications for fairness and equality. Bias in ML algorithms can perpetuate and even exacerbate existing societal prejudices, making it imperative to recognize and actively mitigate biases in ML models. This section explores the origins of bias in ML, from data collection to algorithmic design, and outlines strategies for creating more inclusive and equitable AI systems.

Furthermore, the chapter addresses the paramount concern of privacy in ML, examining how personal and sensitive data can be protected in an era where data is the fuel for AI systems. It delves into the challenges of balancing the data needs of powerful ML models with the right to privacy, discussing technological solutions like differential privacy and federated learning, as well as policy-driven approaches.

This chapter is a crucial exploration of the ethical, societal, and humanistic aspects of ML. It provides a comprehensive understanding of how ML systems can and should be governed with ethical responsibility, designed with an awareness of bias, and implemented with a staunch commitment to privacy. This chapter is essential for anyone involved in the field of ML and AI, from data scientists and engineers to policymakers and business leaders, offering insights and strategies for developing AI technologies that are not only technically sound but also socially responsible and ethically grounded.

14.1 Understanding and Mitigating Bias in ML

Bias in machine learning is a pervasive issue that can significantly skew the outcomes of algorithms, leading to unfair and unethical results. This section is a critical exploration of the sources of bias in ML models, the techniques for reducing such bias, and real-world case studies that highlight successful mitigation strategies. This section underscores the importance of recognizing and addressing bias at every stage of the ML process to ensure the development of fair, equitable, and trustworthy ML systems. For practitioners, policymakers, and stakeholders in the field of ML, understanding bias is not only a technical necessity but also a moral imperative.

14.1.1 Identifying Sources of Bias in ML Models

Bias in ML can arise from various sources:

Data Bias: Often, the most significant source of bias is in the data used to train ML models. This includes historical biases, sampling biases, and biases due to underrepresentation or overrepresentation of certain groups.

Algorithmic Bias: Bias can also stem from the design of the algorithms themselves, especially in the choices made during the model development process, such as the selection of features or model type.

Human Bias: Bias can be introduced by the individuals developing and deploying ML models, often unconsciously, through their perspectives, experiences, and cultural backgrounds.

14.1.2 Techniques for Reducing Bias in ML Algorithms

Several techniques can be employed to reduce bias:

Diverse and Representative Data: Ensure the training data is as diverse and representative as possible. Techniques like oversampling underrepresented groups or using synthetic data can help.

Bias Detection and Correction Algorithms: Utilize algorithms and tools designed to detect and correct bias. This includes fairness-aware modeling and the use of metrics to assess bias.

Regular Auditing: Conduct regular audits of ML models to assess for bias. This should be an ongoing process, as models may develop bias over time as they interact with new data.

14.1.3 Case Studies on Bias Mitigation in ML

Real-world case studies illustrate the successful mitigation of bias:

Bias Mitigation in Hiring Algorithms: An example includes companies using ML for recruitment and implementing fairness-aware algorithms to ensure that candidates are evaluated without gender or racial bias.

Fair Credit Scoring Models: Financial institutions have employed ML models for credit scoring that are regularly audited and adjusted to avoid biases against certain demographic groups.

Ethical AI in Healthcare: Case studies in healthcare show the use of diverse datasets and continuous monitoring to ensure that diagnostic algorithms do not favor one group over another, thus ensuring equitable healthcare treatment.

Understanding and mitigating bias in ML is a multifaceted challenge that requires a conscientious and systematic approach. By identifying the sources of bias, employing techniques to reduce it, and learning from real-world case studies, ML practitioners and stakeholders can work towards developing fairer, more ethical ML models. This effort is crucial not only for the integrity of ML systems but also for the advancement of a just and equitable society where technology serves everyone equally.

14.2 Ethical Considerations and ML Governance

In the rapidly evolving field of machine learning, ethical considerations and governance play critical roles in ensuring that these technologies are developed and deployed responsibly. This section addresses the need for establishing ethical guidelines and effective governance structures to oversee ML practices. This section delves into the creation of ethical frameworks, the role of governance in ensuring responsible ML deployment, and the challenge of balancing technological innovation with ethical responsibilities. For organizations and practitioners in the ML space, understanding and implementing these principles is essential to build trust and maintain the social license to operate in an increasingly AI-driven world.

14.2.1 Establishing Ethical Guidelines for ML Practices

Developing ethical guidelines for ML involves:

Identifying Core Ethical Principles: These might include fairness, transparency, non-maleficence (avoiding harm), privacy, and accountability. Guidelines should reflect these principles in the development and application of ML technologies.

Stakeholder Involvement: Engage a diverse group of stakeholders, including ethicists, data scientists, legal experts, and representatives of affected communities, in the guideline development process.

Context-Specific Considerations: Different applications of ML (e.g., healthcare, finance, criminal justice) may require tailored ethical guidelines to address specific challenges and concerns.

14.2.2 Role of Governance in Responsible ML Deployment

Governance structures are essential for overseeing ML deployment:

Development of Governance Frameworks: Create comprehensive governance frameworks that outline procedures and standards for ethical ML development and deployment. This includes regulatory compliance, risk management strategies, and mechanisms for addressing ethical dilemmas.

Oversight Bodies: Establish committees or oversight bodies responsible for monitoring ML projects, ensuring adherence to ethical guidelines, and making decisions on complex ethical issues.

Transparency and Accountability: Implement mechanisms for transparency in ML decision-making processes and establish clear lines of accountability for ML outcomes.

14.2.3 Balancing Innovation with Ethical Responsibilities in ML

Navigating the balance between innovation and ethics requires:

Ethical Risk Assessment: Regularly assess the ethical implications of new ML technologies and applications. This includes evaluating potential biases, impacts on privacy, and broader societal implications.

Promoting Ethical Culture: Foster a culture within organizations that prioritizes ethical considerations in ML development. Encourage ongoing education and dialogue around ethics in technology.

Public Engagement and Trust: Engage with the public and other external stakeholders to build trust and understanding of ML technologies. Address concerns and communicate how ethical considerations are being integrated into ML practices.

Ethical considerations and governance are fundamental to the responsible development and deployment of ML technologies. By establishing robust ethical guidelines, creating effective governance structures, and carefully balancing innovation with ethical responsibilities, organizations can ensure that their use of ML aligns with societal values and contributes positively to the common good. This approach not only mitigates risks but also strengthens the legitimacy and acceptance of ML technologies in various sectors.

14.3 Ensuring Privacy and Data Protection in ML Systems

The integration of privacy and data protection in machine learning systems is a critical concern in an era where data is both a valuable resource and a potential liability. This section addresses the multifaceted challenges of maintaining privacy in the context of ML, the implementation of robust data protection strategies, and the legal and regulatory landscape governing data privacy. This section is essential for ML practitioners and organizations, highlighting the necessity of embedding privacy considerations deeply into ML systems to safeguard sensitive information and comply with increasing regulatory demands.

14.3.1 Privacy Challenges in Machine Learning

The privacy challenges in ML include:

Data Sensitivity: ML often requires access to sensitive data, raising concerns about unauthorized access and potential misuse.

Model Inversion and Data Leakage: Advanced ML models, especially in deep learning, can inadvertently reveal sensitive data or characteristics about individuals, known as model inversion or data leakage.

Anonymity and De-identification: Ensuring that individuals cannot be re-identified from datasets, especially when combining multiple data sources, poses a significant challenge.

14.3.2 Implementing Data Protection Strategies in ML

To protect data in ML systems, several strategies can be employed:

Data Encryption: Encrypt sensitive data both at rest and in transit. Use secure protocols for data transfer and access.

Differential Privacy: Implement differential privacy techniques in ML models to add noise to the datasets or queries, thereby preventing the disclosure of individual data points.

Access Controls and Auditing: Establish strict access controls for data and ML models. Regularly audit data access logs to detect and prevent unauthorized access.

Data Minimization: Only collect and use data that is necessary for the specific ML task, minimizing exposure of sensitive information.

14.3.3 Legal and Regulatory Aspects of Privacy in ML Systems

Navigating the legal and regulatory landscape requires:

Compliance with Data Protection Laws: Adhere to relevant data protection laws such as GDPR in the EU, CCPA in California, and other regional data protection regulations.

Regular Legal Audits: Conduct regular legal audits to ensure that ML systems comply with the evolving legal landscape regarding data privacy and protection.

Transparency and Consent: Be transparent about the use of data in ML systems. Where applicable, obtain explicit consent from individuals for the collection and use of their data.

Data Protection Officers (DPOs): Appoint DPOs in organizations to oversee compliance with data privacy laws, conduct privacy impact assessments, and act as a point of contact for regulatory authorities.

Ensuring privacy and data protection in ML systems is a complex yet essential aspect of modern ML practices. By addressing the privacy challenges, implementing effective data protection strategies, and complying with legal and regulatory requirements, organizations can safeguard sensitive data and build trust with users. These practices not only protect individuals' privacy but also enhance the integrity and credibility of ML systems in a data-driven world.

Chapter 15: The New Frontiers of Generative AI

Generative AI, a groundbreaking field within artificial intelligence, stands at the forefront of technological innovation, heralding a new era in which machines are not just tools for analysis but partners in creation. This fascinating domain of AI involves algorithms that can generate novel content, be it images, text, music, or even complex simulations, from existing data sets. Unlike traditional AI focused on interpreting and learning from data, Generative AI takes a bold leap forward – it uses learned patterns to create new, original outputs that often surpass the boundaries of human imagination.

At the heart of Generative AI are neural networks and deep learning techniques that have evolved to understand and replicate complex patterns and structures found in real-world data. This capability has unlocked unprecedented potential across various sectors, from art and design to science and engineering. Generative AI is reshaping the creative process, aiding in design and innovation, and presenting new solutions to age-old problems through synthetic data generation and simulation.

However, as we embrace the capabilities of Generative AI, we also step into a realm brimming with ethical considerations and practical challenges. The power to generate new data brings with it questions of authenticity, originality, and the ethical use of AI-generated content. In this chapter, we embark on an exploration of Generative AI – understanding its mechanisms, witnessing its impact across industries, and contemplating the ethical and practical dimensions of this revolutionary technology. This journey into the world of Generative AI is not just about comprehending its technical underpinnings but also about appreciating its potential to transform the landscape of human creativity and innovation.

We embark on this journey by first "Exploring the Capabilities of Generative AI," delving into the depths of how these technologies are not merely imitating but innovating, giving birth to content that is novel, dynamic, and often indistinguishable from human-generated work. From generating art and music to creating realistic text and synthetic data, this section illustrates the diverse and profound capabilities of Generative AI, showcasing how it's reshaping the landscape of creation and invention.

Transitioning to "Impact of Generative AI on Industries," we examine the profound effects of these technologies across various sectors. This part of the chapter takes a closer look at how industries are being revolutionized by the power of generative models. From altering the creative process in the arts to revolutionizing product design, medical research, and beyond, this section paints a picture of a future where Generative AI is an integral part of the fabric of industry, augmenting human potential and opening new avenues for exploration and growth.

Finally, we confront the "Ethical Considerations and Future Challenges in Generative AI." This crucial segment addresses the complex ethical dilemmas and challenges that arise as these technologies advance. Issues such as the potential for misuse, questions of intellectual property, the impact on job markets, and the ethical implications of AI-generated content are explored. This section aims to foster a dialogue on responsible innovation, ensuring that the development and application of Generative AI align with societal values and ethical standards.

"The New Frontiers of Generative AI" is not just a chapter about technological advancements; it's a narrative about the future of creativity, the ethical responsibility of innovators, and the potential for a new era where human and machine collaboration opens up unprecedented possibilities. As we venture through this chapter, we invite readers to envision a world enhanced by Generative AI, marked by an amalgamation of technology, ethics, and boundless creativity.

15.1 Exploring the Capabilities of Generative AI

Generative AI, a subfield of artificial intelligence focused on generating new and original content, has been witnessing rapid advancements and expanding its influence across various domains. This section, "Exploring the Capabilities of Generative AI," ventures into the core of what makes Generative AI a groundbreaking technology. We explore its technological foundations, dive into its diverse applications ranging from art to science, and examine how it's pushing the boundaries and shaping the future.

15.1.1 Technological Foundations and Innovations in Generative AI

Generative AI is built on a foundation of sophisticated algorithms and neural network architectures like Generative Adversarial Networks (GANs) and Variational Autoencoders (VAEs). These technologies enable machines to understand and replicate complex patterns found in real-world data, leading to the creation of new, original content. This section delves into these underlying technologies, discussing their evolution and how continuous innovations are enhancing the capabilities of Generative AI. We also explore the latest advancements in this field, such as improvements in natural language processing and image generation, which have opened new possibilities in AI creativity.

15.1.2 Diverse Applications: From Art to Science

The applications of Generative AI are as diverse as they are transformative. In the realm of art, AI has been used to create stunning visuals, music, and even literature, challenging our traditional notions of creativity. In science and engineering, Generative AI aids in complex simulations, drug discovery, and material design. This section showcases the wide array of applications, illustrating how Generative AI is being utilized in various fields. From generating realistic images and composing music to aiding in critical scientific research, the applications are boundless and continually growing.

15.1.3 Pushing Boundaries: Generative AI's Expanding Horizons

As the capabilities of Generative AI grow, so do its horizons. This part of the section looks at the future potential of Generative AI and how it is set to revolutionize industries and everyday life. We discuss the emerging trends and future directions of this technology, including its integration with other technological advancements, its potential role in shaping future workplaces, and its impact on societal norms and practices. The section also addresses the possible future challenges and opportunities that Generative AI presents, painting a picture of a world where AI's creative potential is harnessed across all aspects of human endeavor.

This section is a comprehensive examination of the technological sophistication, diverse applications, and future potential of Generative AI. This section provides a deep understanding of how Generative AI is not just a technological marvel but a catalyst for innovation and transformation across various domains.

15.2 Impact of Generative AI on Industries

Generative AI is rapidly transforming industries by introducing new capabilities and revolutionizing traditional processes. In this section we examine how this innovative technology is influencing various sectors, from creative industries like art and music to critical fields such as healthcare and business. This exploration offers insights into the profound changes brought about by Generative AI, showcasing its versatility and the breadth of its influence.

15.2.1 Revolutionizing Creative Industries: Art, Music, and Entertainment

Generative AI has made significant inroads in the creative industries, altering the landscape of art, music, and entertainment. In the world of visual arts, AI algorithms are creating paintings and digital art that challenge our understanding of creativity. In music, AI is being used to compose new pieces, sometimes in collaboration with human artists, offering novel sounds and compositions. In the entertainment industry, AI is used for everything from scriptwriting to special effects, opening new avenues for storytelling and production. This section delves into these transformative changes, illustrating how Generative AI is not just an assistant in the creative process but an active participant, reshaping the way we create and consume art and entertainment.

15.2.2 Generative AI in Healthcare: Innovations and Breakthroughs

The healthcare sector is witnessing a surge in the application of Generative AI, leading to breakthroughs in diagnosis, treatment, and drug discovery. AI algorithms are being used to generate synthetic data for research, thereby overcoming the limitations of data availability while ensuring privacy. In diagnostics, Generative AI helps in creating more accurate models for disease identification and progression. It also plays a crucial role in drug development, speeding up the discovery of new compounds and treatment methods. This section explores these innovations, highlighting the potential of Generative AI to revolutionize healthcare and improve patient outcomes.

15.2.3 Transforming Business Landscapes: Marketing, Finance, and Beyond

Generative AI's impact extends well into the business world, transforming areas like marketing, finance, and customer service. In marketing, AI-generated content is being used to create more personalized and engaging customer experiences. In finance, Generative AI assists in risk assessment, fraud detection, and algorithmic trading, bringing in new levels of efficiency and accuracy. Beyond these, the technology is finding applications in various business processes, from automating routine tasks to generating insights from large data sets. This section examines how Generative AI is not just optimizing existing processes but also opening up new possibilities for innovation in the business world.

The section provides a panoramic view of how Generative AI is reshaping various sectors. By showcasing its applications and the resultant transformations, this section underscores Generative AI's role as a key driver of innovation and change in today's industries.

15.3 Ethical Considerations and Future Challenges in Generative AI

As Generative AI continues to advance and integrate into various facets of society, it brings forth a spectrum of ethical considerations and future challenges that need careful navigation. This section delves into the complexities surrounding the ethical deployment of this technology, the risk assessment and management it necessitates, and the sustainability and governance issues it presents for the future. This section aims to foster a deeper understanding of the responsibilities and challenges that come with the innovative power of Generative AI, ensuring that its development and usage align with ethical standards and societal values.

15.3.1 Navigating the Ethical Landscape of Generative AI

The ethical landscape of Generative AI is vast and multifaceted, involving issues such as the authenticity and originality of AI-generated content, the potential for deepfakes and misinformation, and the implications for intellectual property rights. This section explores these ethical dilemmas, discussing the importance of transparency in AI-generated content, the need for clear ethical guidelines, and the role of human oversight in Generative AI applications. It also addresses the challenges of ensuring fairness and avoiding biases in AI-generated outputs, a task made more complex by the often opaque nature of AI algorithms.

15.3.2 Risk Assessment and Management in Generative AI Developments

Risk management is a critical component in the development and deployment of Generative AI. This part of the chapter examines the strategies for identifying, assessing, and mitigating the risks associated with Generative AI technologies. It encompasses the evaluation of potential misuse, the impact on privacy and security, and the risks of unintended consequences. The section advocates for a proactive approach to risk management, including regular audits, the implementation of robust security measures, and the development of contingency plans to address potential issues as they arise.

15.3.3 Future Challenges: Sustainability and Governance of Generative AI

Looking ahead, the sustainability and governance of Generative AI present significant challenges. This section discusses the long-term implications of widespread AI deployment, including its environmental impact, the need for sustainable AI development practices, and the challenges of energy consumption. It also delves into the governance aspect, exploring the development of global standards and regulatory frameworks that can guide the ethical and responsible use of Generative AI. The importance of international collaboration and the participation of diverse stakeholders in shaping these frameworks are emphasized to ensure that Generative AI benefits society as a whole.

This section offers an in-depth exploration of the ethical and practical complexities that Generative AI brings. By highlighting the need for ethical considerations, robust risk management, and forward-thinking governance, this section underscores the importance of responsible innovation in the realm of Generative AI, ensuring its benefits are realized in a way that is ethical, equitable, and sustainable.

Conclusion

As we reach the conclusion of our exploration into the vast and intricate world of machine learning, artificial intelligence, and their applications, it is evident that we stand at the cusp of a technological revolution. Throughout this book, we have journeyed through the foundational concepts of machine learning, delved into the architectural designs and applications, and confronted the ethical and societal implications of these burgeoning technologies.

In the initial chapters, we unpacked the fundamental principles of machine learning, shedding light on the algorithms and technologies that form the backbone of this field. From understanding neural networks to grasping the complexities of deep learning, these chapters laid the groundwork for a deeper exploration of machine learning's practical and theoretical aspects.

As we moved through the book, we ventured into the realms of architectural design and the various applications of machine learning in industries ranging from healthcare to finance. These chapters revealed not only the versatility of machine learning but also its transformative power. We saw how machine learning is not just a tool for data analysis but a catalyst for innovation, driving advancements in fields once thought beyond the reach of computational sciences.

The latter chapters brought to the forefront the human dimensions of machine learning - governance, bias, privacy, and ethical considerations. Here, we recognized that the journey of machine learning is not solely defined by technological advancements but also by the ethical frameworks we build around these technologies. As we continue to harness the power of machine learning, we must also shoulder the responsibility of guiding its development in a manner that aligns with societal values and ethical standards.

Finally, we explored the exciting frontiers of Generative AI, a testament to the ever-evolving nature of this field. Generative AI not only symbolizes the pinnacle of what machine learning algorithms can achieve but also poses new challenges and opportunities for innovation, creativity, and ethical considerations.

This book has been a comprehensive guide through the multifaceted landscape of machine learning and artificial intelligence. As we look to the future, it is clear that the possibilities are as boundless as our imagination and as profound as our commitment to ethical and responsible innovation. The journey of machine learning is ongoing, and its trajectory is as much in the hands of its architects and practitioners as it is in the hands of society that it will inevitably shape and transform. The future of machine learning is a canvas of immense potential, and it is up to us to paint it with the brushstrokes of innovation, responsibility, and ethical consideration.

Notes

Printed in Great Britain
by Amazon